Timeless Prayers for Peace

Praise for Geoffrey Duncan's worship anthologies

Seeing Christ in Others

'Poignant, challenging, profound and helpful'
Methodist Recorder

'An exceptional collection . . . a compassionate resource'
Celebrate

'a treasure store'
Reform

Wisdom is Calling

'a wonderful resource . . . gloriously varied'
Baptist Times

'a timeless anthology . . . Wisdom will be Calling for many
years to come with its voices of hope and agenda for change'
Reform

'enrich[es] and inspire[s] and enlarge[s] our understanding of
what it means to be a Christian in the world today'
Renew

A World of Blessing

'a large, varied and exciting collection of blessing prayers'
Transmission

'Here is a wonderful collection . . . a blessing, a renewal and a
bit of courage on the way'
Daily Mail

'this book is itself a rich blessing'
Reform

Timeless Prayers
for Peace

Compiled by
Geoffrey Duncan

CANTERBURY
PRESS
Norwich

© in this compilation Geoffrey Duncan 2003

First published in 2003 by the Canterbury Press Norwich
(a publishing imprint of Hymns Ancient & Modern Limited,
a registered charity)
St Mary's Works, St Mary's Plain,
Norwich, Norfolk, NR3 3BH

www.scm-canterburypress.co.uk

British Library Cataloguing in Publication data

A catalogue record for this book is available
from the British Library

ISBN 1-85311-515-0

Typeset by Regent Typesetting, London
Printed and bound by
Biddles Ltd, www.biddles.co.uk

Contents

It's a pleasure to dedicate *Timeless Prayers for Peace* to friends and colleagues who work ceaselessly to bring about a better way of life for children and adults who live with various physical and mental impairments. These are the staff of the Association of People with Disability, BasicNeeds India, and Samarthya – Samuha in Bangalore and Vidyasagar in Chennai, south India. Thank you for opening my eyes and enriching my life.

Foreword

These are difficult times for people who believe in peace. Those of us who advocate peace in the midst of these times of 'wars and rumours of wars' are dismissed as starry-eyed idealists, naive and not terribly bright. We are sidelined and ignored. Therefore it is not enough for you and me simply to love peace, we must also be equipped with arguments to support our perspective.

Timeless Prayers for Peace gives us the words we need. It is a collection with roots deep in the Scriptures, and this is perhaps its greatest strength. There is nothing we are facing now that the prophets of Israel and the early followers of Jesus did not know. They plead with us to remember that in times of danger faithful integrity is our most important responsibility. The greater the danger, the more crucial it is that we should hold onto the shalom vision that makes us who we are. This book offers prayer after prayer, reflection after reflection, to remind us.

The book also offers us a community. It can be very lonely speaking for peace! Here are voices, strong voices, from all around the world. They challenge us to live what we pray. They call us to account. They offer a focus for re-commitment should our courage ever falter. We can turn to this book whenever we need the assurance that we are not alone.

And of course, we can use it in worship together. Those who have treasured Geoffrey Duncan's anthologies over the years will welcome this new addition to the collection. Again and again, the fresh words he finds inject new energy and insight into our services. It is an unhappy truth that we human beings can become jaded with even the most profound truths of our faith. The words in this book cut through the weariness of familiarity to grab hold of us in the name of the living God.

I pray that this book may indeed help to reshape the world. It is not too extravagant a hope: our words are powerful, and so are our prayers. May God's Kingdom come; may God's will be done on earth as it is in heaven.

Roberta Rominger
November 2002

Introduction

The Advent season has just started. This is a time for watching ... expectation ... and hope. However, this will also be a time of frenetic activity when patience will be in short supply, especially with the children, as people search for presents in the rush of shopping. Visits will be made, food will be prepared, carol concerts, choir and nativity play rehearsals will be a way of life ... and somewhere at some time, someone will mention the Prince of Peace. Many people have wondered over the years what all this mad rush has to do with peace. I often long for a time of quiet and learn that other people have the same sentiment – somehow we all get caught up in the mad rush.

We cannot escape the fact that today, as in the past, there are politicians and spin doctors who cover up the truth, there are presidents and leaders with very frightening powers, there are people who gain financially by selling arms to countries which are burdened by the shackles of debt, and there are people who prepare for war. Many women and men are forced to take part in battle even though they do not agree with what is happening to them. Families, friends and loved ones will be injured and killed.

All of this confirms my belief that we need to work untiringly and unceasingly with people in faith communities and allied secular organizations in this country and in the global context to promote peace.

I have just returned from Bangalore, south India, working alongside my daughter, son-in-law and many people in the faith communities to bring about a better deal in life for marginalized people who suffer from physical or mental impairment. Many of these people are children, men and women who live in the slums of Bangalore where there is no clean water, no electricity and no toilet facilities. In remote rural areas people live in similar conditions. There are drought-prone areas and hunger is prevalent. They do not have nutritious food and there is no work for the vast majority of these people. This is just one part of the world and one knows that many people suffer in other countries.

Like many other people my day-long prayers are those of being active so that people will come to know peace in their personal lives. Peace of mind is a factor for everyone regardless of who we are and where we live. Each of us is flesh and blood with feelings and emotions as we laugh and cry. Peace should be present in the lives of everyone.

When minds are turned towards peace, and money is used to provide clean water, health and education for everyone, there will be the beginning of one aspect of peace.

As people of faith we need to watch and expect with the hope that there will be the day when justice and peace will reign for humankind. I believe that more people of faith could become activists for peace in its various aspects. For me, to be an activist is to be quietly determined – speaking out, letter writing, joining a peace organisation, participating in a peace rally and letting governments know that the voice of the people for peace is more powerful than the dropping of bombs and promoting weapons of war. These are small but effective ways of working for the day when swords will be turned into ploughshares and nations will not go to war.

I hope that *Timeless Prayers for Peace* will encourage people already engaged in the promotion of peace to continue their commitment, and that people who waver and are not sure if they should be active will be persuaded to join in so that women and men who live in fear, in poverty, with hunger and illness always present, will live in peace and know that justice will flow down like a never-ending river.

Pray for justice and peace at all times.

Peace, Shalom, Salaam.

Geoffrey Duncan
December 2002

Chapter One
Visions of Peace

Visions of Peace
Based on Isaiah 61:1–4

Good News!
God brings the gospel to the poor;
his liberating Christ adore.
Do not refuse
    to hear the Word
that tells the prisoners they are free
the jubilee
    of Christ the Lord.

Good News!
God makes his broken people whole;
he will the guilt of Zion console.
He will accuse
    our age-long sin,
and with a shout of holy joy
that sin destroy
    and victory win.

Good News!
God calls us to proclaim his reign;
to share his love, to share his pain.
As grace subdues
    the powers of wrong,
then with the poor, with one accord
we praise the Lord
with freedom's song.

David Fox
Wales

Peace: A Vision

Then there was peace.
No longer did night's black subdue us
   to unfamiliar horizons;
No longer did death's chill tune us
   to self-doubt and silent torment;
No longer did the east wind shrive
   our bones and shrivel hope;
No longer did our sadness solicit
   canonical laments;
For the panic of undoing was undone
   and dreams we used to know fulfilled.
Even the nations – cautious, waiting for
   deceit – saw it and were amazed,
And laughed with us at children playing
   their perennial games of catch and chase.

But soon peace was turned away.

Now
May it return to us. Imbue our land with
   your design, intent;
Refresh us with barley, rice and butter-milk,
   sweet chestnuts and lemon mint;
Gladden us with springs and rivers, new water
   from wells, wine from evening bowls;
Father here wild marjoram, silky eels,
   buckeye butterflies and determined wasps.
Feed us: as there is earthly meat, may there
   be heavenly bread.
Give us a name and purpose again, pledge prosperity
   and a warming sun.
Then this: grant that we – awkward and
   inconsequent – may catch epiphanies of love.

Derek Webster
England

A Vision of God's Shalom

We praise you our Loving God,
for creating an earth with enough room for everyone,
where nature sustains environments of harmony and balance,
where new life springs out of death and decay,
where adaptation and change bring new possibilities.

We praise you our Loving God,
for the gift of your Son identified with our humanity,
who welcomes the outcast and the lost,
who does not see the world as we see it,
but proclaims peace and justice for all.

We praise you our Loving God,
for the exuberance and wisdom of your Spirit,
who invites us to move on in our journey of faith,
who challenges us to forgiveness and reconciliation,
and sends us out to live our lives as part of the solution.

Clare McBeath
England

A Moment of Peace

Eternal God
Thank you for this moment,
watching the morning sun glinting on the surf,
listening to the waves lapping the shore
I feel and sense your all-creating presence,
I am at one with you and your world.

Inspire and enable me to hold this moment,

when the media bombard my senses
with images of war and its consequences
and I feel powerless and angry,

5

help me to recreate that moment
when I was still,
when I knew your peace.

In the stillness
I pray
for your peace in the world.

Heather Johnston
England

Life . . . Truth . . . Light Persist

In the midst of death
Life persists.
In the midst of untruth
Truth persists.
In the midst of darkness
Light persists.
Hence I gather that God is
Life, Truth and Light.

Mahatma Gandhi
India

Love and Peace

Lord God Almighty, You are true Peace and Love eternal:
enlighten our souls with the brightness of your peace and puri-
fy our consciences with the sweetness of your love, that we
may with peaceful hearts wait for the Author of peace, and in
the adversities of this world may ever have you for our
Guardian and protector: and so being fenced about by your
care may trustingly give ourselves to the love of your peace.
Amen.

Before AD 700
Source Unknown

We Have a Dream

Leader: Almighty God, that your church may become a
prophetic witness for peace,
People: We have a dream.
Leader: That we no longer neglect the word's poor and
needy,
People: We have a dream.
Leader: That we may halt the present moves towards war,
People: We have a dream.
Leader: That we may stop our threats to use nuclear
weapons,
People: We have a dream.
Leader: That we may rely only on the armour of truth,
faithfulness,
love
and the word of God,
People: We have a dream.
Leader: That we build a world for love and human frailty,
People: We have a dream.
Leader: That we may hope in the face of despair and
brokenness,
People: We have a dream.
Leader: That we may grow in faith and awareness of the
resurrection at work within us,
People: We have a dream.

Source Unknown

You Can't Break My People's Spirit
On watching a film about racial and religious hatred.
'Love your enemy,' Jesus said.

You can't break my people's spirit
by the hatred of your words.
Love is greater than that hatred,
makes your shouting seem absurd.

7

I am black, I'm gay, I'm Jewish,
all the labels that you hurl
fit my person, frame my visage,
lit by flames that writhe and curl.

Kristallnacht will be remembered
as the shards explode around,
but in debris and disorder
we know courage can be found.

We're no longer running from you,
now we turn and face to face
we will love you through your hatred,
we will make a loving space.

We will grow beyond that hatred
to the peace that is required
for us all to live together
as a family, love inspired.

Andrew Pratt
England

Choose a Life of Non-violence

God, we want to choose a life of non-violence.
Help us to hiss, but not to harm;
to hear the Voice that calls us Beloved;
to be compassion within compassion within compassion;

to choose right action, not results;
to throw star after star against a dark sky;
to stretch out our hands and reach what we cannot.

Give us the strength and courage
not only to believe but to act;
to recognize our own participation in violence

and our need for conversion;
to challenge the unjust and violent structures of our day;

to gather, time and again, around the table in dialogue;
to create and promote peaceful alternatives wherever we are;
to continue to be a voice and witness of non-violence.

Our journey through the Doorway to Peace
Begins with the step we choose to take today.
Be with us. Guide us.
Love us into your Love beyond measure.
Amen.

Mary Lou Kownacki
USA

Peace in the World

If there is righteousness in the heart, there will be beauty in
    the character;
If there is beauty in the character, there will be harmony in the
    home;
If there is harmony in the home, there will be order in the
    nation;
If there is order in the nation, there will be peace in the world.

Confucius

Break Your Sword

Do not fear,
He who fears hates,
He who hates kills.
Break your sword and throw it away.
I have been delivered from desire and fear,
So I know the power of God.

Mahatma Gandhi
India

Be Blissful and at Peace

All in this world are my friends, I have no enemies – let the whole universe be blessed; let all beings be engaged in one another's well-being; let all weakness, sickness and faults be diminished and vanish; let everyone, everywhere, be blissful and at peace.

A Jain Prayer
India

They Reply 'Peace'

Those who are closest to Allah's heart are those who walk gently on the earth and when the ignorant address them as 'fool' they reply 'peace'.

A Muslim Prayer

May All Beings Be Happy

In safety and in bliss, may all beings be happy.
Whatever beings there may be, be they weak or strong,
Excepting none; short, tall or middle-sized,
Large or small, seen or unseen,
Dwelling far or near, born or yet to be born,
May they all be happy.

A Buddhist Prayer

Love

That one I love who is incapable of ill will, who is friendly and compassionate. Living beyond the reach of *I* and *mine* and of pleasure and pain, patient, contented, self-controlled, firm in faith, with all heart and mind given to me – with such a one I am in love.

Not agitating the world or agitated by it, but standing above the sway of elation, competition and fear: my beloved.

Detached, pure, efficient, impartial, never anxious, selfless in all undertakings, my devotee, very dear to me.

Who runs not after the pleasant or away from the painful, grieves not, lusts not, but lets things come and go as they happen.

That devotee who looks upon friend and foe with equal regard, who is not buoyed up by praise nor cast down by blame, alike in heat and cold, pleasure and pain, free from selfish attachments, the same in honour and dishonour, quiet, ever full, in harmony everywhere, firm in faith – such a one is dear to me.

Bhagavad Gita
India

For the Healing of the World

Let there be the Word of God,
in every heart impearled.
The living Word
is told and heard
for the healing of the world.

Let there be the Love of God
in Jesus Christ unfurled.
The cross of death
gave life its breath
for the healing of the world.

Let there be the Wind of God.
Through all times it has whirled.
The Spirit moves,
reviews, renews
for the healing of the world.

Let there be the Church of God,
committed, true and bold.

11

The bread we share
in deed and prayer
for the healing of the world.

Per Harling
Sweden

An Alphabet for Peace: Wisdom Sayings

Arrogant evil, flourishing in the place of honour,
    quickly dies as dry bark in winter's fires.
Believe in God, let your eyes love him
    and his silent word will home in your heart.
Commit each hour of life to him and your
    integrity will shine as a midday sun.
Don't brood when evil is victorious, trust in him,
    know that patience opens his gates.
Eventually evil will be conquered; then look up,
    see children playing under his white sun.

Faith will sustain you when wickedness triumphs;
    remember, to the meek is promised an inheritance.
God mocks the cunning schemes of the wicked
    and laughs at the sharpness of their snares.
Helpless, the poor are threatened; then God
    breaks the weapons of sin in sinner's hands.
I know that the need of the innocent
    is worth more than the gold of the guilty.
Just as the Lord loves the blameless, so in
    broken times he will care for his people.

Know this: wickedness is like spring greenery
    which soon shrivels to summer's dust.
Lend to the unreliable and lose the loan,
    but see the blessed give graciously to the needful.
May you walk the Lord's way; on his path
    a rounding love will protect and guide you.
Never in all my years have I seen the good

12

abandoned by God, pleading for bread.
Offences are now forgiven; look up and see the place
of awakening where you shall be with love.

Peace will dwell with justice, evil men will be forgotten;
the good will endure to receive their summer dreams.
Quiet and true, the virtuous are hosts to wisdom,
the voice of holy reason reigns in their lives.
Responsive to his will and obedient to his call,
the righteous know the kingdom of the heart.
Sinners seek the lives of the good, yet God
will not let them perish in that fire without light.
Trust the Lord, walk his way and
your joy will be hope for his love.

Unworthy men feast but briefly in their airy villas,
the tree's shadow lengthens, they are seen no more.
Virtuous people and their families walk in the light,
in the procession of those whom the Lord loves.
Wickedness and those who practise it
will be forgotten, as if they had never lived.
Expect comfort and blessings from the Lord,
even when there are trials and splinters on your way.
Your refuge is the Lord, know that
he longs for you in your longing for him.
Zeal for God motivates the holy, they are not lost
for they stay in the secret place of his love.

Derek Webster
England

God of Love and Love Abundant

God of Love and Love abundant,
we give thanks for all your care
you are making hate redundant;
you give love enough to share!

13

Love of Life and Life abundant,
born with grace to be mature
God is making death redundant;
God gives Life that can endure!

Life of Hope and Hope abundant,
boundless probability
God is making fear redundant;
God gives hope that sets all free!

Hope of Peace and Peace abundant,
reconciliation done
God is making war redundant;
God gives peace that heals each
one!

Peace of God and God abundant,
guaranteeing every good
every evil now confounding
With intended familyhood!

Tune: St Catherine

David J. Harding
England

Whatever Your Race, Your Colour or Creed

Whatever your race, your colour or creed
you are a sister or brother to me.
You speak with a language I don't understand
but I want to learn what you mean.

So much we could share if you listen to me,
so much if I listen to you.
Wherever you're from, whatever your need,
however you name God, whatever you plead,

your culture is foreign, unusual to me
but both of us want to be free.
    Whatever your race . . .

So much we could share if you listen to me,
so much if I listen to you.
When tragedy strikes and our lives spin around,
while babies are crying and battle resounds
I still know you love me, and I still love you,
I'll help with what you need to do.
    Whatever your race . . .

So much we could share if you listen to me,
so much if I listen to you.
So let's join together, the table is set,
the laughter and pleasure will help us forget
the fear at the difference that keeps us apart.
In loving we'll make a new start.
    Whatever your race . . .

Tune: 11.8.10.11.11.8 and refrain

Andrew Pratt
England

Look Into a Person's Eyes

One day, a young fugitive, trying to hide himself from the enemy, entered a small village. The people were kind to him and offered him a place to stay. But when the soldiers who sought the fugitive asked where he was hiding, everyone became frightened. The soldiers threatened to burn the village and kill every person in it unless the young man was handed over to them before dawn. The people went to their minister and asked him what to do. The minister, torn between handing over the boy to the enemy or having his people killed, withdrew to his room and read his Bible, hoping to find the answer before dawn. After many hours, in the early morning, his eyes fell on these words:

'It is better that one man dies than that a whole people be lost.'

The minister closed his Bible and called the soldiers and told them where the boy was hidden. And after the soldiers led the boy away to be killed, there was a feast in the village because the minister had saved the lives of his people. But the minister did not celebrate.

Overcome with deep sadness, he remained in his room. That night an angel came to him and asked, 'What have you done?' He replied, 'I handed over the fugitive to the enemy.' Then the angel said, 'But don't you know you have handed over the Messiah?' 'How could I know?' replied the minister anxiously. The angel said, 'If, instead of reading your Bible, you had visited this young man just once and looked into his eyes, you would have known.'

Source Unknown

Lions and Cows

Lord, in the day of your coming
there will be reconciliation.
The wolf and the lamb will play;
the leopard and the goat will enjoy harmony;
lions and cows will eat grass together
and children will play safely with them;
babies will pick up snakes without harm.
The whole world will be a place of peace
in the day of your coming.

John Johansen-Berg
England

A Universal Meditation

May all beings be happy,
May all beings know joy.
May all beings know peace of mind and body,
May all beings know health and harmony,
May all beings know love and compassion,
May all beings be blessed
And attain to their supreme goal.

Jim Pym
England

Pray for Ourselves

Pray not for Arab
or Jew
or Palestinian
or Israeli
but pray rather
for ourselves
that we might not
divide them in our
prayers but keep
them both together
in our hearts

Based on a prayer of a
Palestinian Christian
Christian Aid
England

Propaganda

Those of us who love peace must organize as effectively as the
war hawks. As they spread their propaganda of war, we must
spread the propaganda of peace.

Martin Luther King
USA

Peace Is . . .

Peace is the resolution of conflict
as we make our peace.

Peace is the struggle for harmony
as we live in peace.

Peace is being set free from anxiety
as we are left in peace.

Peace is our Christian calling
as we share the Peace.

Peace is our blessing from worship
as we go in peace.

Peace is God's final resolution
as we rest in peace

Marjorie Dobson
England

Amazing God

Amazing God, your world is vast and wide and we are only a
very small part of it.
Yet our world, however small, expands to fill our whole
horizon and encloses us within it
to keep us contained and comfortable.
Open our eyes to larger visions and to the way that all our
lives interconnect
in a world
which appears to grow smaller by the minute.
We are all your family, wherever we are.

Marjorie Dobson
England

All Thoughts of Truth and Peace

Almighty God, from whom all thoughts of truth and peace proceed:
kindle, we pray thee, in every heart the true love of peace, and guide with thy pure and peaceable wisdom those who take counsel for the nations of the earth; that in tranquillity thy kingdom may go forward, till the earth is filled with the knowledge of thy love; through Jesus Christ our Lord. Amen.

Francis Paget
(1851–1911)

Love to All

Now may every living thing, young or old, weak or strong, living near or far, known or unknown, living or departed or yet unborn, may every living thing be full of bliss.

A Buddhist Meditation

To Be More Loving

Help me, O Lord, to be more loving. Help me, O Lord, not to be afraid to love the outcast, the leper, the unmarried pregnant woman, the traitor to the state, the man out of prison. Help me by my love to restore the faith of the disillusioned, the disappointed, the early bereaved. Help me by my love to be the witness of your love. And may I this coming day be able to do some work of peace for you.

Alan Paton
(1903–88)

A Franciscan Prayer for Peace

Lord, make me an instrument of your peace,
Where there is hatred, let me sow love,
Where there is injury, pardon,

Where there is doubt, faith,
Where there is despair, hope,
Where there is darkness, light,
Where there is sadness, joy.
O Divine Master, grant that I may seek
not so much to be consoled as to console,
to be understood as to understand,
to be loved as to love,
for it is in giving that we receive,
it is in pardoning that we are pardoned,
and it is in dying that we are born to eternal life. Amen.

St Francis

God of All Creation

God of all creation,
of all that live in soil, in seas and air,
you weave with great variation
the web of life, so fragile, still so fair.
Give us knowledge,
that we may mend it.
Give us wisdom,
that we may tend it.
Give us love and true compassion,
that we may care for all your life.

Per Harling
Sweden

Flowers in the Desert

Loving Creator, you will pour out your blessing
and the desert will blossom with abundant flowers;
the wilderness will become fruitful
so that your people may be filled with joy.
The blind will see; the deaf will hear;
the lame will jump around with happiness.

From dry ground springs of living water
will flow in abundance.
For your people the time of sorrow will be over;
they will sing songs of joy and peace.

John Johansen-Berg
England

Live a Day at a Time

Live a day at a time
is the clear command of the Lord.
For us, just now, he knows
that just this day is quite enough.
Lord help us plan this hour
as we can live this minute,
leaving the rest to you.
Next week, next month, next year
your rule of love and peace
will surely come
in ways we least expect.
Those times are yours
and so are these
and so are we.

Christine and David J. Harding
England

A Daily Prayer for Peace

Grant peace, happiness, blessing, grace, loving kindness and
mercy to all humanity. Bless us, Our Father, one and all with
the light of your countenance and enrich us with life, loving
kindness, righteousness, blessing, mercy and peace.
May it please you to bless all peoples at all times and in all
places with your gift of peace.

Jewish Daily Prayer Book
(adapted)

Thanks to God

Thanks to God
for the language of love,
for the struggle for peace,
for the witness to truth,
for justice and mercy,
for death and new life,
as we know them in our lives,
and through the life of Jesus Christ.

Janet Lees
England

Hands

There are hands, that are offered as help to a friend,
others, that take, but they never will lend.
There are hands, gently stroking their lover´s soft cheek,
others, that always are willing to beat.

Open your hand to the gift of my hand,
by warming each other united we stand.
Only by trusting and sharing we see
the meaning of life as God meant it to be.

There are hands, that receive every day what they need,
others, that keep what they have in their greed.
There are hands, that are open to feel and to touch,
others, that – clenched – will be ready to crush.

Open your hand . . .

Hands are mouth to the deaf and are eyes to the blind,
hands may untie or they may only bind.

22

People's hands may be speaking the language of trust,
being the means of the good and the just.

Open your hand. . .

Per Harling
Sweden

Faith in God

A living faith in non-violence is impossible without a living
faith in God. A non-violent man can do nothing save by the
power and grace of God. Without it he won't have the courage
to die without anger, without fear and without retaliation.
Such courage comes from the belief that God sits in the hearts
of all and that there should be no fear in the presence of God.
The knowledge of the omnipresence of God also means respect
for the lives even of those who may be called opponents.

Mahatma Gandhi
India

Compline

Be present, O merciful God, and protect us through the silent
hours of this night, so that we who are wearied by the changes
and chances of this fleeting world, may repose upon thy eternal
changelessness; through Jesus Christ our Lord.
Amen.

From the Anglican Rite of Compline

The Fruits of Peace
Based on Galatians 6:7–9

The fruit of Silence is Prayer,
The fruit of Prayer is Faith,
The fruit of Faith is Love.

The fruit of Love is Service,
The fruit of Service is Peace.

Mother Teresa
India

Three Steps of Grace

Three steps of grace – that lead to Thee
Three steps to take – up to Thy tree
The Step of Faith – I do believe

The Step of Hope – myself receive
The Step of Love – that one step more

O Risen Lord – Thee I adore.

Source Unknown

Work for the Peace of the City

Work for the peace (the shalom) of the city . . . pray to the Lord on its behalf, since on its peace yours depends . . . (Jeremiah 29:7 NJB)

In 586 BCE Jerusalem was laid waste by the Babylonian army under Nebuchadnezzar. The majority of the population, including all the professional classes, were taken into exile in Babylon. A short while later Jeremiah wrote to the exiles urging them to settle down in Babylon, build up the life of the Jewish community there, and (astonishingly) to work for shalom, the peace and well-being, of Babylon.)

Peace to the city,
shalom for Babylon.
Peace to the Temple desecrators
and the exile-makers,
shalom on the zigurrat of the sun-god and those who believe
    that his is the true reality.

24

Surely you don't mean it Lord?
Surely your blessing is for us, your faithful few?

My child, love your enemies and pray for those who persecute
    you.
Hatred diminishes
envy poisons
and fear cripples,
your peace and theirs are one.

But Lord,
we are your chosen ones,
elected to walk in your path
and they have dragged us from it,
severed us from the umbilical cord of the Temple,
quenched the fires of sacrifice.
How can you ask us to pray for peace?

My child,
I weep with you by Babylon's waters
for my heart is broken by your pain,
yet my tears flow too for those who
dominate and destroy,
blind to my light
deaf to my symphony,
caught in spirals of delusion and violence.

You,
my weak ones,
my little ones,
can craft their salvation from your steadfast vulnerability.
Your peace and theirs are one.

So be it Lord,
hear our prayer for mighty Babylon
for our peace and hers are one
in your rich economy of your blessing.

Lead us to the land of milk and honey
where lion lies with lamb and ox with bear,
and Babylonian and Jew party together
in the light of a rainbow
and a boy baby lies in the arms of a mother distracted by
   crosses.
Amen.

David G. Cornick
England

Jubilate!

Jubilate! God is loving
everyone and everywhere,
taking issue with the wrongful,
giving hope to those who care.
Jubilate! Jubilate!
Long live life! We have to share!

Jubilate! Love is peacing
discords into harmony.
We expect to see Love's
blessings
stretching into infinity.
Jubilate! Jubilate!
Life is loving constantly!

Jubilate! War is over
giving way to peace at last!
We expect to see war's horror
relegated to the past.
Jubilate! Jubilate!
War, expelled, is fleeing fast!

Jubilate! Peace is present,
gift for the new human race
as a present for the future

ever more God's gifted grace.
Jubilate! Jubilate!
Every peace is now in place!

David J. Harding
England

Challenged to Reconcile

A sermon preached at Women's World Day of Prayer 2002

'I want them all destroyed!' This cry by an Israeli woman broke
through the relative and comfortable peace of my living room
early one evening just a couple of weeks ago. 'I want them all
destroyed!' was the spine-chilling cry reported via satellite to
people's living rooms the world over. 'I want them all
destroyed!' was the desperate reaction of a grief-stricken Israeli
mother whose young son had just been killed in a Palestinian
attack.

Her cry for revenge and justice and look of total despair is
etched for ever on my memory. 'I want them all destroyed!'
'Them', not other women's children, or grandchildren, not
someone's husband or wife. Not someone's sister or brother, or
mother or father. But 'them', the faceless, nameless enemy.

The material for this Women's World Day of Prayer is written by a group of women who know and understand that cry
all too well, written by women from many different ethnic
minorities, from many different denominations, from many
different backgrounds. The 'challenge to reconcile' comes to us
from a context of division, discrimination, pain and distrust.
The 'challenge to reconcile' comes to us from a situation of
poverty and economic decline. And it comes from a group of
women who have put aside their differences and risked much
in order to be reconciled to one another.

So what does this challenge have to say to us today?
Everywhere we look in the news there are references to
September 11th. September 11th has become one of the most
memorable dates in history. 'Life will never be the same again!'

27

'September 11th has changed the world' – so we are told. Or has it?

The world has always been a violent place. History is full of atrocities, of war, of senseless destruction. We base our faith on a Bible which if it was turned into a screenplay I would not let my children watch – it would be at least a certificate 18. The Bible does not pretend that violence doesn't exist, does not edit out the parts we'd rather forget. Rather, the Bible holds together both stories of violence and stories of reconciliation – stories of war and stories of peace. And over time as the faith story of the Hebrew people is told, we see the gradually unfolding message of God's vision of peace and harmony between all peoples.

In the early days, the God of the Israelites is understood as a nationalistic God, a God on the side of the Israelites as they destroy other nations and claim land for themselves. But as the story unfolds through the judges, the prophets, and the wisdom writers a different emphasis, a different challenge begins to emerge. No longer is God only a national God, but God is understood as being concerned for the outsiders, for those from other nations.

'I want them all destroyed' is one very powerful and disturbing voice. But it is not the only voice. It is not the only response to a world of violence and war. The women of Romania have put aside their differences in order to challenge us in the churches to be reconciled. Their challenge is to the Christian church to put aside its differences in order to work together for peace and justice. But I think the challenge is bigger than that. The challenge is broader than the Christian churches. For me, the real challenge is to reconciliation across the divisions of religion or race.

September 11th hasn't changed the world. The thousands of deaths are catastrophic but a tiny number when compared to the needless deaths every day from hunger, poverty and disease across our world. September 11th hasn't changed the world, but it has shaken the dominant western capitalist view of the world and exposed the other side of consumerism and a deep-seated racism towards those of other faiths and particularly towards the Muslim world. But the war in Afghanistan is not the only response to September 11th.

In America, a small group of people have started to communicate with one another. Started to express their unease. Started to speak in the language of peace not revenge. This group is made up of some of the relatives and friends of people who died in Washington and New York. They are a group who have come together to say that they do not want the memory of their loved ones to be tainted with calls for revenge and violence. They are a small but nevertheless significant voice challenging us all to reconciliation.

In a story recorded in the book of Samuel, Abigail lives out this challenge to reconciliation. Like many women she is a wise woman, an intuitive woman who senses the danger and threat of violence. She challenges us to be wise, to recognize the signs of violence in our society.

Abigail, like many women, is a woman of strength and courage. She dares to walk the path of non-violence, to face the dominant power empty-handed. She is creative and draws on her inner resources in order to protect her family. She challenges us to take a creative stand against injustice and violence.

Abigail, like many women, is a faithful woman. She believes in a God of peace and justice, a God who will inspire and walk alongside her. She challenges us to listen again to the stories of faith that call us to work for reconciliation.

Abigail, like many women, is also a prophet. She speaks to the future king, preventing him from taking revenge and challenging him to walk a path of peace and reconciliation. She challenges us to name the violence and injustice in our society and to challenge our leaders to make peace not war.

So where does this challenge leave us? The women of Romania and the relatives of those who died on September 11th seem a very long way from us. We seem insignificant in comparison. How can what we do make a difference?

Last autumn a friend who teaches at a local school asked my family and me to go with her to an Indian food festival held at the local Islamic mosque. She had been invited by the parents

29

of one of her pupils and told to bring her friends. We turned up to the smells of all sorts of wonderful dishes being cooked, to the spectacle of a water-melon eating contest and to the sounds of Indian music. We were very warmly welcomed and fed to bursting by our hosts who had never met us before.

My friend and I had our hands painted with henna while a couple of women watched over my sleeping toddler. The children on the bouncy castle made sure that he was not crushed by the bigger children and helped him down when he'd had enough. And above all we were invited to look around the mosque and to ask questions.

As we took off our shoes and entered the main room of the mosque a woman greeted us warmly. She told us that after the events of September 11th the Muslim community wanted us to know that their faith called them to peace not violence, called them to be reconciled not to make war. And they opened up their most holy, sacred place in order to demonstrate their desire to break down the barriers between different religions and between different races, to show that Allah is a God of love.

Does our faith not also challenge us to do the same? Does our faith not also challenge us to reconciliation? Look around our communities and we can see there is much work to be done? Do we know our next door neighbours or the family down the street? Have we as churches thought about how we can make refugees and asylum seekers, exiled from their own homes and lands, feel welcomed in this community? Have we challenged the authorities to set the appropriate services and support structures in place?

The stories I've told this morning are all stories of ordinary women. Wise women, courageous women, faithful women and prophetic women, but ordinary women. We too are ordinary women, wise women, courageous women, faithful women and prophetic women. Will we take up the challenge to reconciliation here in our own community and in the wider world?

Clare McBeath
England

Is This A Place Where Games Are Played?

Written in response to an interfaith meeting held in conjunction with the Methodist Conference in Wolverhampton UK , 2002 and led by the Wolverhampton Interfaith Group

Is this a place where games are played,
where hidden schemes are subtly laid;
or is there now an openness
where mutual love puts fears to rest?

What if your face has different lines
traced over years, through different times
in places I have never been,
brought on by pain I have not seen?

Within humanity we share
a need for strength to offer care.
To build up love we take our stand.
If we are one, give me your hand.

Andrew Pratt
England

God Help Us

God, help us understand,
    that we can only enter your peace
when we have released the tools of war.

God, help us know,
    that your peace is a choice
we must make through our actions.

God, help us believe,
    that your peace for all
is an attainable dream.

God, help us see,
   that in peace we do not lose control,
but gain one another.

God, help us speak,
   that others may know
your promise of peace.

God, help us hear,
   that the truth of your peace
is told in many ways.

Louise Margaret Granahan
Canada

The Sapling
Inspired by Goethe's Gefunden

Out strolling down the winding path
That passes through the forest
I came across a seedling spruce
Pushing its way through unrelenting tarmac.

'What chance have you,' I thought,
'Of growing into a tree of beauty and of use?
I leave you there and you will die,
Half-grown, unnoticed, valueless.'

So bending down I prised it out,
Drew it from its barren bed,
And in Corrymeela let it sink its roots
And mix with other trees.

How many of our young people,
Conditioned, captured, caged,
Must think in strictly party lines,
Throats throttled if they venture out of step.

Lift them from that hard tarmac
Of bigotry and hate,
In new surroundings stretch their roots,
Expose their minds, give them a proper chance.

So through the years in spite of fears
Another generation will be born
To save our land.

Kathleen Davey
Northern Ireland

A Peace Dream

I dream
Of a loving world
Where we see each other
With God's eyes;

I dream
Of a resourceful world
Where we cherish the unique gift
Of each other;

I dream
Of a hopeful world
Where we recognize the power of God's grace
To transform and make new;

I dream of peace.

Claire Smith
Guyana

A Blessing
Adapted from Philippians 4:7

The peace and security of God
which passes all our understanding
   and all our human skill,
keep our hearts and minds,
   our whole being,
in the knowledge and love of God,
   which is our path to life,
and in the faith of his Son,
   our Lord Jesus Christ
   who is our Saviour.

Bernard Thorogood
Australia

Chapter Two
Circles of Protective Peace

Weave Your Blessings

Weave your blessings into our lives, dear Lord.
Weave in your open-heartedness so that we can accept others.
Weave in your gentleness so that we can care for others.
Weave in your attentiveness so that we can listen to others.
Weave in your goodness so that we can find good in others.
Weave in your love so that we can love others.
Weave in your blessings into our lives, dear Lord.
Day after day fill us with your Spirit
   and renew our sense of calling
   as followers of Jesus,
   and servants of your Kingdom.
Amen.

Neil Thorogood
England

Let Nothing Disturb You

Let nothing disturb you;
nothing dismay you;
all things pass,
but God never changes.
Whoever has God lacks nothing:
if you have only God, you have more than enough

Teresa of Avila
(1515–82)

Circles

I like to think of life in circles,
The earth itself, the sun,
The pathway of the planets, of the moon,
The horizon seen from a mountain top.

The Celtic 'caim' drawn through the air
Depicting God, the encompasser
The Chinese 'yuan', united and round,
Their Autumn Family Festival.

What have we done to our circles on earth?
To the circle of family life?
Or the families built into communities?
Or the nations' round table talks?

You can't draw a circle just out of the blue
Without a fixed central point,
Until we can find it right at the heart,
We can never complete the arc.

But once we have found it, our eyes can turn in
To the centre, our arms stretch out wide
To those on each side of us, offering support,
While receiving from them in return.

Kathleen Davey
Northern Ireland

The Dove

One olive tree above the flood
and one branch is the sign
of solid land again.
You bring hope, messenger of peace.

What olive leaves do we discover
in the world's flood of pain?

The fall of a dictator,
a pact between old enemies,
a government halving its spending on arms,

a family embracing different cultures,
a doctor's care in a war-torn land,
and children with uncorrupted eyes.

Jesus of the olive grove
you knew the agony of doubt.
Shall we be saved?
Yes, in the garden dawn;
Yes, in the upper room
and yes, where the tree of life
bears leaves to heal the nations.

Bernard Thorogood
Australia

Olive, Acharavi

Trunk wrinkly and wriggly,
olive oozing with love,
offering a leaf to the dove

olive cooking and lighting
olive for wood, shade and food,
on the quiet slope where the road

flagging the valley bends gently
between the mountains and dark, thin, tall,
cupressus pillars in its wind uphill.

Backcloth for dancing, the man
bringing down fodder on
a donkey, the woman tethering goats,

it oils thought, matures
silence, celebrates equilibrium,
hears the accordion head the walk to the wedding

sits it out in all weathers,
subject to netting, fruits quietly,
ripe or not, bitter at first.

Brian Louis Pearce
England

Village Wedding

Couple and priest circle the altar
Just as the dancers circle the couple:
They might be dancing before the ark.

Dancing at the feast in the mountains
Circling the ancients and the timeless olives
Heading dance and procession

To accordion, guitar, violin,
Laughter, clapping of shepherds,
Glittering, circling all night

Clasped ikon to ikon, in Nimfes,
Holding hands, keeping silence
Handing each other the cup.

Brian Louis Pearce
England

What Is Peace?

Peace, says the grandmother,
is rocking a small baby,
and time stands still,
and nothing matters but
her presence in your arms
and the small movements

keeping her safe and contented
half awake half asleep.

Barbara Moss
England

Peace Is Like Gossamer

Peace is like gossamer –
vulnerable, yet indestructible:
tear it, and it will be rewoven.
Peace does not despair.
Begin to weave a web of peace:
start in the centre
and make peace with yourself
and your God.
Take the threads outwards
and build peace within your family, your community
– and in the circles of those you find it hard to like.
Then stretch your concern
into all the world.
Weave a web of peace
and do not despair.
Love is the warp in the fabric of life:
truth is the weft:
care and integrity together –
vulnerable
but ultimately
indestructible.
Together,
they spell
peace.

Kate Compston
England

This Is the Place

This is the place
Where death meets life,
Where sorrow is present,
Where hard questions are asked
And not always answered.

This is the place
Where pain is felt,
Where partings are made real,
Where holy words
Can ring empty and hollow.

This is the place
Where we ask, 'Why?'
Where we cry, 'What now?'
Where God is near,
Or feels so far away.

This is the place
Where emotions are mixed,
Where tears are shed,
Where memories return
Of brighter yesterdays.

This is the place
Where God says, 'I know.'
Where God says, 'I am here.'
Where God sheds a tear
Along with us.

This is the place
Where God understands,
Where God stands and waits,
Where Jesus says,
'I went through it.'

This is the place
Where Easter is hope,
Where eternity is God,
Where each ending
Becomes a beginning.

This is the place
Where God is all around
And very much alive
Because we need him
Here in this place.

Marjorie Dobson
England

Peace Comes With Every . . .

forgiving word
sincere welcome
refused war
clear understanding
universal truth
signed treaty
gentle treatment
honest thought
friendly smile
forgiven sin
forfeited revenge
granted reprieve
angry protest
accepting prayer
compassionate person
conscientious objection
family meal
attentive listening
just law
merciful judgement

wistful hope
social healing
shared good
reconciling gesture
kindly gift
non-violent experiment
peaceable endeavour
proper disarmament
restrained deed
new day
open community
twinged conscience
patient concern
achieved ceasefire
harmless behaviour
failed aggression
harmonious achievement
loving action.

David J. Harding
England

I Am a Man of Peace

I am a man of peace.
I believe in peace.
But I do not want peace at any price.
I do not want the peace that you find in stone;
I do not want the peace that you find in the grave;
but I do want the peace that you find embedded
in the human breast,
which is exposed to the arrows of the whole world,
but which is protected from all harm
by the power of Almighty God.

Mahatma Gandhi
India

Forgive Us, Lord

Forgive us, Lord, the selfishness
that breaks Your peace:
the wounded pride, the jealousy
that finds release
in shattering others' calm.

Forgive us, Lord, the empty prayer
for peace on earth,
so loudly spoke, so little felt;
we shrink the birth
of Christ-like sympathy.

Forgive us, Lord, the weakened will
that rests content
at peace while justice is denied
and lives are rent
by inhumanity.

Lord, give us now the inner peace
for which we pray,
and by your love give strength of mind
to win a day
when all are reconciled.

Stephen Orchard
England

I Find Peace

in a warm, strong yet gentle hand
Enclosed in a tightly curled rosebud
By the sight of a rainbow
I am held   Firmly, in a loving embrace

in the knowledge I am accepted
Enclosed by encouragement
Simply for ever
I am safe   Because I am loved

in the choices I make
Enclothed with God's power
To do my Maker's will
I am free   To be the best I can be

by your body in my neighbour
By your spirit in your love
I am touched   By your work through all creation

Content, I find peace

knowing I am held, I am safe, I am free
Held by my Creator
Safe with my Saviour
Freed by the Spirit

Judy Gunthorpe
England

Deep Peace

Deep peace of the quiet earth to you.
Deep peace of the shining star to you.
Deep peace of the Son of Peace to you.
Deep peace of the heart of Mary to you.
Deep peace of the flowing air to you.
Deep peace of the rolling wave to you.
Deep peace of the bright blue sky to you.
Deep peace of the Prince of Peace to you.

Traditional Celtic Blessing
Source Unknown

The Cost of Peace

Branxton Hill is a most peaceful place. Two miles south of the Scottish border in Northumberland, United Kingdom, it looks towards the lush pastures of the Tweed valley. It was not always so. In 1513 some fifteen thousand Scots and English died in one day, by sword and arrow, in the pitched Battle of Flodden. Now all there is to remind us of that carnage is a text carved in stone 'To the brave of both nations.' It is set on a cross. The cost of peace is often far too high – the passion of Christ places that costliness even within the heart of God.

Stephen Platten
England

Peace Is Flowing Like a River

We sing 'Peace is flowing like a river . . . flowing out though you and me'.

But is it really like that for you?

I can't remember when it felt like that for me!

Often peace eludes me: in the midst of a toddler's tantrum; when jostling with fellow travellers to get on the train; if facing an unruly, noisy class of teenagers; or stuck in traffic congestion with horns blaring.

Peace seems very far away.

Yet . . . within that noise, pressed by a crush of people, assailed by someone's emotions, frustrated by delay – there is the gift to switch channel, to focus inwards, to centre my thoughts.

And there I find calm, I am bathed in peace – my energy revives. In that moment of need my spirit is fed.

And peace is flowing like a river.

Judy Gunthorpe
England

Web of Peace

Peace is as delicate
as the woven web of the spider;
so intricate, so complex,
yet so easily destroyed.
Lord, give us the peace that lasts,
that binds us together,
that gives hope.
Peace, so delicate yet so strong,
is our prayer for today and tomorrow.

John Johansen-Berg
England

A Cry for Peace –

A Dalit Prayer

God of all
It's so hard to live on the margins –
Lonely and forgotten,
Despised . . .
Despondent . . .
Remember me,
Put back my confidence
Restore my dignity
And walk down the edges with me . .
.

Then knowing you, Lord,
I shall rise . . .
Rise in hope.

Church of South India
Diaconal Ministry

Your Peace

Lord, I am troubled, lonely, defeated.
Calm my restless heart as you stilled the sea.
Let peace, your peace, flow through me like a river.
Let your mighty love flow out through me.

Roger Grainger
England

Seeking Peace

Lord Jesus, I longed for peace so I went into the hills, to a place where skylarks sing and there are no buildings, no people. I sat on a stone and gazed to the west: there was only a sea of purple heather. I gazed to the south: I saw only heather. I looked eastward and saw the heather and beyond, the real sea, blue and sparkling in the sunshine. I felt myself enfolded in peace, caressed by peace.

But then, Lord, I looked to the north, and saw, far in the distance, black smoke polluting the pale sky. I thought of the poor who live near those factories, whose houses are grim, whose health is failing. I knew I could not hold on to my precious peace, and I remembered how you took friends away in a boat to find rest from the crowds, but the people discovered you, so you took pity on them because they were like sheep without a shepherd, and set yourself to teach them.

Lord, thank you for showing me the heather and the sea . . . and the smoke.

Anthea Dove
England

Jesus My Peace

Jesus, bear us on in
Your heart, into the
Heart of the Father
That he may give us
In you
To his children who
Long for you our Peace

Jesus my Peace
May I so
Hold you in my heart till
I am held in
Your heart
And become
Your Peace

May the God of
Cloud and broad
Sedge and flint
The Source of
Sea and brook
Give you his
PEACE

Revd Mother Sheila CAH
England

Be Still

Be still
And let God's peace wash over you
Like waves lapping over pebbles
Smoothing rough edges of insurmountable worries
To tiny insignificant grains of sand,
Taking away the jaggedness of sin

To leave smooth shining love.
And let the peace of God,
The Father, Son and Holy Spirit
Be with you all today and every day.
Amen.

Lesley K. Steel
Scotland

Circle(s) of Peace

May the love of the Creator enfold you
May the joy of the Saviour surround you
May the power of the Spirit fill you
May the peace of the Father, Son and Spirit
encircle you now and always.

God of the sparkling stars, give us peace;
God of the radiant moon, give us peace;
God of the bright sun, give us peace;
God of the vast universe, give us peace.

God of grace and love,
through our childhood you give us joy;
in our middle years you give us happiness;
in the evening of life you give us fulfilment.
In life, in death, grant us your peace.

In the mirror I see my reflection;
looking down at still water, more reflections;
reflections in silver and steel;
but when I look at the face of Christ,
the radiance brings both peace and joy
and I long to reflect that peace for others.

There is the moment when noise ceases,
the time when the busy world is quiet,
the evening when the day's work is done,

the time when a struggle is ended.
In that moment I find peace;
in that silence I know your presence, Lord,
your presence and your peace.

Weaver God,
weave your joy into our lives;
bind us together in unity of purpose;
make us in the pattern of your love.
Weaver God,
weave your peace into our being.

John Johansen-Berg
England

Peace Enfolds Creation

Peace enfolds creation
as a mother cradles a child.
Peace chastises oppression
which threatens the unity of the family.
Peace rejects injustice
since it disturbs the common welfare.
Peace brings forgiveness
where there has been deep hurt.
Peace heals creation
as a mother soothes her baby.

John Johansen-Berg
England

An Evening Prayer for Peace

Lord God of the falling dusk
Creator of time and space
Thank you for the day that has passed
for tasks completed, for goals achieved

Forgive us for any misuse of our time

Grant us your peace in the hours of night

Christ of the setting sun
Source of light and love
Thank you for the day that has passed
for friendships renewed, for relationships formed

Forgive us for any conflict we have caused

Grant us your peace in the hours of night

Spirit of the wild goose
Giver of power and peace
Thank you for the day that has passed
for comfort and strength in times of need

Forgive us for ignoring the cries and needs of others

Grant us all your peace this night.

Heather Johnston
England

God, When I Look into Your Eyes

God, when I look into your eyes
I fathom such devoted love,
you penetrate my deepest need,
you close around me like a glove.

They said that we could never meet,
my sexuality denied
the right that others flaunt and show,
their words of arrogance deride.

But I am confident, O God,
that you will love me as I am;
that no one in their human pride
can block your love, can build a dam;

For I am yours, and you are mine,
I'm gay, I'm free, accepted, strong,
and no one now will put me down,
I'm favoured, loved, and I belong.

Andrew Pratt
England

Focusing

Shall I focus on these iron bars
pitted and rusted, caging me in,
resented yet familiar,
or shall I look beyond blurred bars
to where a field of buttercups
mirrors and holds the sunlight
even on cloudy days,
and children gather armfuls
to put in jam jars on some windowsill
reminders of a carefree, happy hour?

But farther still, past bars and buttercups,
and distant hills,
focus on infinity,
I see and know
freedom and peace at last.

Helene McLeod
England

The Earth Is Holy

The Earth is Holy,
it is the Lord's.
In love we come together to proclaim the
Good News that speaks
of a quality of life
that is
freedom in justice,
   freedom in peace,
freedom to breathe,
   freedom to plant,
freedom to walk without fences,
      freedom to be at home on our own land.

We pray that we may be instruments of
God's peace and justice.

Source Unknown

The Wind, the Water, the Weather

Why does the wind blow?
Bringing on its waves
The white dove of peace

Why does the water rain down?
Bringing on its waves
The white dove of peace – the Paraclete

Why does the weather storm?
Bringing on its waves
The white dove of peace – the Holy Spirit

On the soft wings of a white dove
You arrived at Iona – Holy Isle –
Columbine, St Columba.

Gabrielle Hopkins
England

At the Ocean

The ocean stretches
Into the sky,
Placid streaming
To eternity's end;
Retreat after the
Tempest of
Bullets, blows
And words.

The ocean stretches
Into the sky;
Gentle lapping
Lullaby
Soft music midst the
Cries that cannot be stilled
That are not heard.

The ocean stretches
Into the sky;
Refreshing salt-sea breeze
Soothing spirits torn
In equal-space struggle
With those who
Grasp it all.

The ocean stretches
Into the sky;
Like meets like

In union
Giving hope,
Reminder of God's
Promised peace.

The ocean stretches
To the sky;
Peaceful rest.

Claire Smith
Guyana

Larksong

I hear the skylark trilling
above the Surrey* downs
singing it seems in ecstasy,
and if I close my eyes
the lark I hear is singing
far, far away from here.
And I am walking the hills again,
or sitting by the shore
as the waves roll up the white sand,
in the clear light,
the shining light
and the deep peace of Iona.

Pour out your soul in ecstasy,
lark of the Surrey hills,
lift me up into your ecstasy
to leave this self behind.
Take me away to that thin place,
far, far away from here
where earth and heaven come very close

* *A county in southern England*

that my soul may be renewed
and my empty heart be filled again
with the clear light,
the shining light
and the deep peace
of Iona.

Helene McLeod
England

Prayer of the Jains

May I never cause pain to any living being,
May I never utter untruth,
And may I never covet the wealth or wife of another.
May I never drink the nectar of contentment . . .
May there be mutual love in the world,
May delusion dwell at a distance . . .
May all understand the Laws of Truth and joyfully
sorrow and suffering endure.
Peace,
Shanti.
Peace.

One of the Founders of Jainism

Waiting

Waiting and watching –
Hoping and praying,
Patience and worry,
Hopes and fears,
Smiles and tears,
Loneliness and hugs,
Sleepless nights and exhausted days.

Waiting and watching –
Emotions and confusions.
The mind races with possibilities
That dare not be expressed.
Eyes meet, tears start,
Averted looks, embarrassed faces –
How to respond?

Waiting and watching –
Heartache and hope,
Helplessness and action,
Shock and acceptance,
Dreams turned to nightmares,
Jumbled days and nights –
Has life changed for ever?

Waiting and watching –
God knows the pain.
God knows the wretchedness
Of watching those we love.
God knows the heartache
Of being powerless to help.
God knows the cost of living and loving.

God knows,
God shares,
God cries,
God cares.
God's arms are strong to hold our weakness,
His presence is peace to receive our fear,
And his patience and strength
Are there for us –
Always.

Ruth Sermon
England

It Had a Tune

A memory from childhood with a twin brother who has died

When silence came
it had a tune –
greensong, pure greensong,
a bird, intent, unforced,
contained in the freedom of birds.

Rooks in the trees at West Ham House,
swaying – they had a tune too,
grating itself into time,
into boys' memories
of wide grass, and clumpy nests way up,
dens, woodfires and baked potatoes.

That's how it is now,
fixed and flowing
down a valley
a valley down which I'm still walking

by myself now.

When silence came
it was filled
it had a tune.

Geoffrey Herbert
England

Window

The grass is singing in a frenzy at the wind,
We're bending, almost breaking with your whipping:
will we stand it, will we survive?

The land is weathered wise and changes the song:
Wind, you've worn me, and sun, you've dried me.
I'm still here, my brown hills and my hard rocks
are my memories of your ancestors.

The sea hurls its words in the breakers
and spits them in the spray:
I'm the eternal ocean. Wind, I allow you
to surf on my back and ski-jump over cliffs.
and wear the land and tear the grass.

The sky spreads its dark blue wings down
over the songs, and eagles them away.

We saw this through our window and heard the songs.
In here it's quiet, gentler than the land and wind and sea.
The window will help us go out again into the wild air,
to be their neighbours and sing our songs with theirs.

Geoffrey Herbert
England

Your Pilgrimage

May your pilgrimage take you
along the shores of Galilee,
through the garden of Gethsemane,
and on the heights of transfiguration.
May you not fear the valley of darkness,
nor be troubled by the storms at sea.
May the companion of the Emmaus road
open the Scriptures to you
and bring you peace.

John Johansen-Berg
England

A Prayer of a Desperate Parent

God of quiet and serenity,
Grant me patience as I tend to the morning chores
And the baby is screaming.
Encircle me with your calm as I try to concentrate on written
    work
And the baby is screaming.
Enfold me in your peace as I continue on the daily round
And the baby is screaming.

Ah! My prayers are answered. She sleeps!
Peace, perfect peace. (At least for a while)

Zam Walker
Wales/Scotland

Spirit of Life

Spirit of Life,
Shed your light where there is darkness;
Spread your truth where there are lies;
Bring your freedom to defeat oppression;
Share your love where there is hate.
Let your peace overcome all enmity,
so that the garden of creation
may bloom with a thousand flowers
and the varied people of planet earth
may be sustained by your creative energy.

John Johansen-Berg
England

Together

Together, God in us, in human life,
Creating us, in our uniqueness,
Uniting us in our solidarity,
Supporting us in our suffering,

62

Holding us in our belonging,
Cradling us in our vulnerability,
Accepting us in all our nakedness,
Seeking us in our searching for peace,
Together, God in us, in our humanity.

Frances Ballantyne
England

We Need Your Mother Love O God

We need your mother love O God to keep and hold us tight,
We need your mother love O God to lead us through the
  night.
We need your Holy Spirit to comfort and to guide,
May she give us courage to do what is right.

We need your mother love O God to teach us how to live,
A love that never forces but draws because it gives.
May we reject the pride that thinks we are the best
And that we deserve much more while others can have less.

We need your mother love O God to teach us to say no
To all the ways of violence, to all the ways of war.
Forgive us for the way we have supported evil deeds
Done in the name of our nation while we've simply kept our
  peace.

We need your mother love O God to teach us to say yes
To all the ways of beauty, to all the ways that bless;
To be gentle with creation and all God's creatures too,
To treat the earth with kindness, to cherish and renew.

We need your mother love O God, so we're numbered with
  the meek.
Forgive our need to dominate over poor and weak,
And men over women and race over race;
Forgive us for the fear that hides the human face.

We need your mother love O God to keep our spirits true
To the values of your Kingdom, to the attitudes from you.
Blessed are the merciful, blessed are the meek,
Blessed are the humble, blessed are the weak.

We need your mother love O God to keep and hold us tight,
We need your mother love O God to lead us through the
　　night.
We need your Holy Spirit to comfort and to guide,
May she give us courage to do what is right.

Garth Hewitt
England

The Lord Our God Will Be Our Guide

The Lord our God will be our guide,
We trust in his protection;
We walk in safety by his side,
We shall not be forsaken.
As long as life shall last,
His power will hold us fast;
What danger shall we fear,
When his strong arms are near
to shield us from temptation?

Though wandering in delusion's night,
Men choose the ways of evil;
Turning their backs on God's true light
to bargain with the devil.
They disobey God's will –
Pervert, destroy and kill;
Filled with their own conceit,
They scorn the ways of peace,
and fill the world with terror.

Yet still from hell a song shall rise
to fill the world with gladness;
The song of hope, that never dies,
defying hate and madness.
From anger, fear and strife
still springs the tree of life;
Through pain and grief we feel
Christ's hands outstretched to heal
and bind the broken-hearted.

God's word is spoken, strong and sure,
to every generation;
His promise stands for evermore –
We are his new creation.
The Lord of space and time,
Who shares love's bread and wine,
Lord of the open tomb,
Still claims us as His own,
And draws us into heaven.

Jill Jenkins
England

Dealing with Differences

Patient and persistent God,
be present with each one of us
in this meeting.

May we offer our opinions
honestly and openly
and listen attentively
to opposing points of view,
without closing our minds
to the possibility of compromise or change.

May we speak with sensitivity,
not holding the floor too long,
shouting down those who see things differently,
showing impatience with those who are slow
to grasp our point,
or need time to collect and articulate their thoughts.

May we see our own subjectivity
as well as that of others,
and be equally willing to reconsider
or set it aside.

And if we cannot compromise,
may we register our dissent
with dignity and without disrespect,
voting according to our conscience
and not with our feet.

Patient and Persistent God,
may your peacemaking presence
be with us in this meeting,
in all our debate and discussion,
and remain with us when we go home.

Jean Mortimer
England

A Paraphrase of Christ's Prayer

O God of sky and God of Earth
We honour your presence
Within us and beyond.
As we eat may we share your gifts
Of hope and compassion
With all the life of Earth.

Give us, O God, forgiving hearts
Affirming each other
With humour and with grace.
May the lessons from pain and joy
Empower us for spreading
Your just and loving peace.

You greet us here and everywhere
In moments of oneness
And spaces of delight.
To all this we now say Amen.
Your song is our anthem
Your dance is our cosmic joy.

Tune: Creative Love

W. L. Wallace
Aotearoa New Zealand

Museum

So quiet here, in this hide,
step the soft treads of my
own soft feet through my blood.
The sun steals in for a
bit of hush from outside.
I write. Time drips on my
open leaf.
All's still, the mood
sans clamour. Amphora

and pot hold the past, stop-
per the oils of the race,
secrete the future. Room
here for a few old sticks
to put out buds still, pop

in for a nip o' peace, trace
fossils in all the bloom
around them. The clock ticks

on in them. Time charms the
room quiet round them. I sit
as one of them, lost to
the old bustle, to find
lost worlds creaking, hear the
traffic of quiet a bit
after the rush to be through
from cradle to past mind.

Brian Louis Pearce
England

The Powder and the Spark

Tucked down amongst tree and mound,
St Peter and Paul stand rebuking
the cloverless dark. Nettled stone
and wort knit the sojourning
archangel and rogue in duetting
tryst, foil dust's predatory hound.

The hermit Powys took root here, found
the unvisited place, the spooking
quiet, the being left alone,
the thing he wanted, learning
to be one with earth, forgetting
heart's wine, in heat for the mound.

He stayed if God wasn't around,
he sat here when God wasn't looking:
when his entourage had gone
off to lunch or were earning

an honest penny, out-sweating
Adam on Mappowder ground.

Jack came, to leave profoundly affected, but found this booking
of grave space, talk on the bone,
not to his taste, discerning
grace in the dark, the fretting
only penitent's prayer's sound.

He sat here and found God abound-
ing, the bubbling idea cooking –
creative, redeeming – born
out of leazed pax: he saw the burning
but unconsumed window, setting
match to soul-powder, clay bound.

Brian Louis Pearce
England

Come to Me

I pass through the automatic doors
Of the supermarket.
It takes no effort on my part, Lord.
No pushing or pulling, no straining or heaving.
As I draw near – so they glide smoothly open.

'Come to me,' you said.
'Draw near.'
Your arms are open like those doors,
And into your love I walk.
The gates of the city of heaven – New Jerusalem,
As described in your Word,
Are always open.
All I need do is draw near.
I do not have to convince you or impress you.
You call it grace.

Show me, Lord, the opportunities
To walk through all the open doors
Of grace
You place before me
Today.

Martin Wallace
England

Heavy-laden

Why is it Lord
That this bus
Designed to transport adults,
Assumes we only need a tiny space
For our legs
As we sit,
With no space at all
For our heavy bags of shopping?
'These shopping trips will be the death of me!'
I overhear from the large overburdened woman
Behind.

You take me back to the story in the Bible
When the Israelites who carried the Ark of the Covenant
Containing the Ten Commandments on blocks of stone
Stumbled under its heavy weight
And a man call Uzzah steadied the Ark
And fell dead,
Overcome by the weight of the fear of the Lord
Through having touched that holy object.

Our secular lives are so easily stifled
By the compression and the weight of daily living.
Our spiritual lives are so easily stifled
By the compression and the weight of fearful hearts.
I hear you say gently and simply,

'Come unto me you who are heavy laden
and I will give you rest,
even on a bus.'

Martin Wallace
England

Spirit of the Living God
(additional verses)

Spirit of the living God,
Dwell within this place.
Speak within our songs and prayers,
Pass with us the peace.
Warmly, dearly, gladly, freely.
Spirit of the living God,
Dwell within this place.

Spirit of the living God,
Send us out to serve.
Guide our hands and feet each day,
May your words we speak:
Softly, caring, gently sharing,
Spirit of the living God,
Send us out to serve.

Tune: Living God

Michael Jacob Kooiman
Canada

All Will Be Well
Based on the words of Julian of Norwich

All will be well, all things shall be well!
This is the peace of the deep blue dream
This is the light of divinity,
This is the flow of love's healing stream.

All will be well, all things shall be well!
Deeper than pain lies buried delight,
Deeper than grief dwell life's joyful songs,
All of our wounds can nurture new light.

Now is the time to dance heaven's dance,
Time to discern eternity's face,
Moment of knowing beyond all sight,
Day of God's smile and tender embrace.

Tune: Julian

W. L. Wallace
Aotearoa New Zealand

Protecting Spirit

You hovered like a huge bird at the
earth's creation, mothering the planet
as it came into being. You nurtured its
fragile life like a hen settling on a nest,
keeping warm the new life forming
beneath her.

Though the world is centuries old,
Protecting Spirit, we need you now as
ever, to mother our planet, to give
nurture and protection to life which
remains as fragile as if a day old.

Spread your wings across the world.

Enfold each place with your love,
love, freeing, not stifling,
love, exposing us to life's realities, not
then wrapping us in cotton-wool,

love, questioning, shouting, crying and
demanding, not speaking in sweet
nothings and sugary sentimentality.

Enfold each place with your peace,
peace, bringing justice,
not just an absence of war,
peace, demonstrating solutions
for all people, not just the powerful,
peace, recognizing that the earth belongs to God
and that every part of the land is sacred.

Enfold each place with your joy,
joy, reflecting the diversity
of cultures and faiths,
joy, uniting people
through our shared humanity,
joy, overflowing with the fullness of
life that Jesus promised to everyone.

Protecting Spirit,
enfold us with your love, your peace
and your joy, today, and always.
Amen.

Lindsey Sanderson
Scotland

Benediction

May the peace of God,
   our Creator,
whose love is beyond
   the boundaries of our world,
be as close to you as every breath and heartbeat.

73

May the peace of Christ,
    our Redeemer,
whose love walked on earth
    and still walks among us,
strengthen you to walk each step with him.

May the peace of the Spirit,
    our Sustainer,
whose love works in
    and through us,
inspire us all to works of humble magnificence.

Louise Margaret Granahan
Canada

Chapter Three
Peace on Earth

Peace to the World

Peace to the world
Peace to the city
Peace to the village
Peace to the desert
Peace to Mother Earth
Peace to cosmos
Peace to you
Peace to me
Peace to my neighbour
Peace to my enemy
Peace to whom it may concern
Peace, Peace, Peace!

Elizabeth Tapia
The Philippines

Peace and Love

Sons and daughters of a single mother,
Why do you kill one another?
Embrace and care for each other
So that peace and love may be the order.

Josephine Moseray
Sierra Leone

Peace Finds Expression

Creator God,
your peace finds expression
through the artist's brush, in form and colour,
by the sculptor's skill, in curve and line,
in the musician's art, through chords and harmony.
Your peace comes to us
through the poet's pen and novelist's imagination,
by needlecraft and embroidery's finesse

and in all the creative talents of your people.
In such ways may we seek your way of peace
and give glory to your name in all the earth.

John Johansen-Berg
England

O God of Peace

O God of peace, whose peace is Christ your Son,
Put on your armour that the war be won,
The war on war, your Word against the gun:
Allelulia! Allelulia! Allelulia! Allelulia!

O God of power, whose power appears so weak,
Enlist your soldiers from among the meek,
Who won't turn tail but turn the other cheek:
Allelulia! Allelulia! Allelulia! Allelulia!

O God of Love, whose love casts out all fear,
Disarm your people while the warlike jeer,
But rather insults than their blood and tears:
Allelulia! Allelulia! Allelulia! Allelulia!

O God of hosts, whose host is bread of life,
Feed us by faith for strength in times of strife,
And fill with hope the grieving child and wife:
Allelulia! Allelulia! Allelulia! Allelulia!

O God of time, whose time is always nigh,
Keep us alert to leaders' lethal lies,
Come now your reign when truth will never die.
Allelulia! Allelulia! Allelulia! Allelulia!

Tune: Sine nomine

Kim Fabricius
USA

Pax

Pax offered and received
in a hand taken,
in fellowship restored,
blessing a body shaken

Pax in the bread broken,
offered each to each
in and through Christ, as token
of the healed breach

Pax in the wine poured
and taken together:
self-giving Creator adored
crushed in the press, our all-weather

Pax boxed but to rise, glow
like felt light in the mind,
streaming through its stained window,
translucency Passion has signed

Pax in the common lot, fraught
muddle and bustle, mix
of slow-lane and airport,
a traffic-lamp our pyx

Pax in the mart of wits
where souls are tossed and flayed:
pax in the infill pits
where the Lamb bleats, afraid

Pax in the pestful hot-spot
that frustrates all mankind
if, calm amid uproar and riot,
good will works peace of mind

Pax in the flowers, no match
for pax when the bombs fall:
pax that is more than hopscotch
or fainites while factions brawl

Pax that foregoes arboured ease
between thyme and old man
to offer itself like a breeze
that bursts with love but breathes on.

Brian Louis Pearce
England

Lord, Your Peace Disturbs Us

Lord, your peace disturbs us
more than any war,
wrecks complacent living
opens every door.

Christ, your peace is given
now that we may give
to your war-torn people
better ways to live.

Lord, your peace condemns us
for we have not seen
how far from your set-up
'Christian' ways have been.

Lord, your peace empowers us
with sufficient right
to reject all violence,
seeing love is might.

Lord, your peace inspires us
calmly to engage
in the roughest battles
for a gentler age.

Tune: Dungarven – Christine and David J. Harding

David J. Harding
England

Community of Peace

Work us together as contrasting colours,
Join us together across divides of differences,
Bind us together with loving connections,
Unite us together combining our strengths,
Knit us together in patterns of worship,
Pull us together demolishing our barriers,
Mould us together retaining our personhood,
Cement us together softening our bitterness,
Design us together to be communities of peace.

Frances Ballantyne
England

A Prayer for Peace

In the green time of history,
Before the sun was broken,
Our children laughed,
The land was impatient
To give grapes and herbage.

You smiled on us,
Original among peoples;
Smeared the sky with rainbows;

Forgot your anger and
Hid wrath in a far place.

Smile again, pierce faith's obscurity;
Cherish us, repair our madness;
Strip us for freedom.
Come: wed peace to justice,
Mesh goodness and love.

God hears this supplication and speaks.
I will make you blazons of light,
Conscripts of glory. You shall hear
Afresh words that bring salvation,
Know the creative pulse of peace.

No longer will you trespass between
Promise and fulfilment, for I will walk
With you. The invisibility of eternal
Love will come to kiss each new-born
Child and embrace your generations.

Derek Webster
England

Voices for Peace

Tomorrow's children cannot plead
nor the long-suffering earth protest
against today's destroyers;
nor can our forbears cry,
whose sacrifice and toil,
whose vision and whose faith
helped to create the fragile good
that we today enjoy

the fragile good
we could so easily destroy
either by fear, or folly, or mistake.

Only through those who see and care today
the past, the future, and the earth itself
can find a voice,
can plead for peace and life.
Dare we give them a voice to use?
Dare we refuse?

Basil Bridge
England

Give Peace to Your People

Loving God,
Give peace to your people
and inspire us to offer peace to each other.
May we work together to right all wrongs;
may we walk together to protest against injustice;
may we live together seeking the welfare of all
and may we find in your presence
the inner peace that sustains all living beings.

John Johansen-Berg
England

Finding Peace

Stop

Breathe

Smile

Thank you – Thank you – Thank you

The earth – The sky – The moon and the stars –
The wind and the rain

may your true presence embrace me,

breathe me

– Smiling –

just being in the present moment

walk on peace

peace is every step – every step is peace.

Val Philpott
England

Flower of Peace

God of Peace, of Mercy and Love
    may the Flower of Peace
        bloom in the desert of war and adversity
            now and always.
                So be it!

Elizabeth Tapia
The Philippines

A Psalm of Peace

Gracious Spirit, I cry to You
From the depths of my heart.

My country longs for peace
Because she is torn by war
And her children are maimed
By landmines and hunger.

My people cry for justice
How long, O Lord, how long?

Reading the world news makes me
Feel depressed and powerless
Fear starts to immobilize me and my neighbours
Threats of nuclear war and bio-terrorism
Cross our borders.

Why, oh why, has life become so cheap?
Why have people become more vulnerable than before?

Oh, Compassionate God,
Grant me, grant us, discerning spirits,
Courageous and humble hearts;

Cleanse us of all toxic emotions and evil thoughts
Vanish our fears
Strengthen our wills
Answer our prayers
Listen to our dreams.

I dream of a world filled with peace based on justice
I dream of war-free zones and discrimination-free nations
I dream of travelling without fear
I dream, I cry, I hope, I pray.

Divine Spirit, Bathala
Empower us with your Wisdom and Love
So we may learn to choose
The path of righteousness and harmlessness,
Climb the mountain of truth and the ridge of forgiveness.

To turn instruments of war and hatred
Into instruments of peace and reconciliation
To bless all creatures with a smile and loving kindness
To dance the dance of life boldly through the night.

From the depths of my heart
Gracious Spirit,
I dance for You!
So be it!

Elizabeth Tapia
The Philippines

The Nature of Peace

*Words of commission for a person who will live and work for a
peace-living world*

The warmth of understanding
radiates
from a lively gaze
confirming
the unspoken words
'there are many of us who have confidence in you'.

The nature of peace
radiates
from a loving action
confirming
the unspoken words
'continue to be courageous; be who you are'.

The resilience of love
affirms
– in a resolute way –
that you will continue your activist journey
with all the women and men
who serve humankind.

The determination for peace
will assure
people in war-torn lands
that your compassionate spirit

will guide you in your efforts
for peace for all people.

The determination for peace
  must radiate,
    must permeate,
   must shine,
      through adversity
        to give confidence
        and hope

to suffering women and men
on this earth
now . . . today . . .

Geoffrey Duncan
England

Daisy Bud

A few days before Christmas
In a crack in the concrete
Blasted by sleet and hail
An ordinary scarlet-stained daisy bud
Quietly announced
Spring is coming.
Peace is coming.

In spite of the blasting
In spite of the frosty words
In spite of the concrete slabs
Peace will come.
For the tear-stained hearts
Of the ordinary people
Announce it.

Kathleen Davey
Northern Ireland

Where Homes Lie in Ruin

Where the streets are destroyed
and homes lie in ruins,
God, show your mercy
and challenge the culture of war.

Where children beg in the streets,
having no family or home,
God, show your mercy
and challenge our helpless indifference.

Where peace is restored
so that people can return to the their homes,
and shops can open,
God be praised
for what human resilience can achieve.

Where lovers and parents
and children and friends
laugh for pleasure and joy in each other's company,
God be praised
for the miracle of love.

God of Deborah,
who restored trade and safe travel to a war-torn community,
whose story was gossiped by the women as
they drew water in security once again,
and who challenged the members of her community
who stood aloof,
help us to value peaceable pleasures,
keep us faithful in prayer and partnership
and may we never stand aloof from the
requirements of the human community.

Janet Wootton
England

We Hope to God that Wars May Cease

How can we sing a song of peace
when all God loves is scorched by war?
How dare we now confess our faith,
when guarded by things we deplore?

    Because we sing of peaceful means,
    outmatching all that violates,
    of ways of peace so well expressed
    in all the Christian celebrates!

How can we sing a song of joy
where victims over victims mourn?
How dare we here maintain our hope
where right is wronged and wholeness torn?

    Because we sing the joyful truth
    that violent ways are obsolete,
    that gentle Jesus has the wit
    to make God's purposes complete!

How can we sing a song of love
while disregard and hatred last?
How dare we claim a future life
while murderous ways are far from past?

    Because we sing love's new-found tune
    (by discord-makers much despised)
    of rights restored and wrongs forgiven,
    Creation safely harmonized.

We gladly sing: love, joy and peace!
We hope to God that wars may cease!
We celebrate: Christ is the Way,
The Truth and Life . . . for all . . . today!

We gladly sing: love, joy and peace!
We hope to God that wars may cease!
We celebrate: Christ is the Way,
The Truth and Life . . . for all . . . today!

Tunes: Tallis's Canon (verses 1, 3, 5, 7)
Morning Hymn (verses 2, 4, 6, 8)

David J. Harding
England

The Gospel of the Cross

The north-western boundaries of the Republic of Georgia encompass Abkhazia. Riven by ethnic violence it was the centre of a civil war following the independence of Georgia with the dissolution of the Soviet Union. The Abkhaz people were supported by other Caucasian ethnic groups, notably the Chechens. Hatred of Georgians seemed equal among Chechen and Abkhaz alike; the decapitated heads of Georgians were used as footballs during the civil war. Less than ten years later thousands of Chechens, fleeing from Russian tanks, took refuge in the Pankisi Gorge in north-east Georgia. Within days of the first refugee camps being established, young and old aid workers poured into the Gorge with humanitarian aid. They were not Muslims like the fleeing Chechens but Christians – both Orthodox and Baptists from Georgia gave from the bottom of their hearts. The gospel of the cross reaches deeply into humanity – far deeper than any immediate feelings of revenge.

Stephen Platten
England

Epitaph for Ground Zero, Anywhere

The terrible weight has gone.
Sift our silence in the dust,
see our speech in sun-shafts.

Stand still and hear our last word:
Because of us,
let no one else be crushed.

Geoffrey Herbert
England

A Return After Conflict

Like homing bees, sunset-spangled,
We are returning. Without you, kisses are lost,
Eyes unrewarded and there is no heart's ease.

With you, we will laugh at corncrakes,
Sing with the wishes of our children and
Delight that what has been can be again.

Translucent sacraments: conch and cowrie,
Calligraphy of leaves and wings, are
Flecked with glory and feed us with joy.

Through deeps and darks we travel to you.
Our road rejoices with us. Now its uplands
Unfold to the spindrift and greens of paradise.

Know my ardent longing for your breath.
Shade the secret recess of my spirit with your
Shy presence – pivot of life, measure and love.

The past is present with us; your love is our future.
Always remember us: we remember you always,
Pivot of beauty, whirlwind of giving, death of dying.

In our houses, sharing stories of hurt, of
Peace, we will wait before you and adore, sensible
That we are overtaken, overthrown by love.

Derek Webster
England

Remembrance Day

Howls of wind screech through the cracks,
Rain, belching from leaden skies
Pelts like bullets on the plastic dome.
Noise, disturbance, clash of wills.

Inside the curved white walls
Of the little Croi
A silence,
As a score
Or maybe more
Of people drawn from sundry parts
With hearts wounded and bruised
From lifetime buffetings and hurts
Assemble to pray.

The pale, wavering flame
From a lone candle
Gathers together their imploring prayers
And drifts them heavenwards.

The bread and wine are blessed.
Each unto each passes the plate, the cup,
Remembering not only that first time
Our Lord had done the same
And given us the trust to do likewise,
But thinking back in pain
Of those who lost their lives
And of those ones left behind
Whose lives will never be the same.

Heaven and earth are full of Your glory.
Backwards in time our minds can see
From earliest days those faithful few
Who – high and low – met to break bread.

The unseen cloud
Of those who have gone before
Surrounds us,
Lifting us from the slough,
Assuring us this is the harbinger
Of the world as it should be,
Where rich and poor, east and west
Clasp the other in embrace
And say: *The peace of Christ to you.*

The whole wide world of earth and heaven
Past, present and future too
Are linked together in this common act.
Refreshened and renewed
We leave the silence of the Croi,
More able now to face the storm outside.

Kathleen Davey
Northern Ireland

This Is a Day of Remembrance
From a sermon preached on Remembrance Sunday 2001

This is a day of remembrance

Remembrance is an act which 'calls to mind events and people of both past and present'. It is a time when we remember all those who have given themselves for others . . . given their lives, their minds, their physical labour, their hopes and their fears.

Memories are powerful, they make us into the people we are today and help us to relive our experiences, linking us with the past. But memories are more than simply dwelling on the past. They are our link with the future, our way of learning the lessons from the past in order to guide us in our living in the present. Memories are the source of our hopes and vision of a better world for our children and our children's children.

93

This is a day of remembrance

Re-membering not only helps us to live in the present and orientates us towards the future, it is also the opposite of dis-membering. Re-membering is 'a putting together again', healing, reconciling. The biblical story of Ruth shows us God's concern for the dis-membered in our society, God's concern for the poor, the disabled, the women, foreigners, widows. It is not a story about international relations, or war, or about the rich and powerful. It is not, unlike many of the other Old Testament stories, a story about the anarchy of the time of Judges or a story about the establishment of the monarchy. It is a story about the lives of ordinary people, a story about survival, loyalty and generosity.

We also remember Mark's story of the widow who puts her two coins in the temple collection box, who gives not out of her wealth but out of her poverty. Even her two small coins count. Yet again, Jesus undermines the religious leaders of his day. 'Beware of the scribes who parade around and take the best for themselves – beware of the ones responsible for the care of the poor, the vulnerable, the widows, they are crooks who claim God is on their side.'

The gospel is subversive. It shows Jesus, time and time again, remembering the poor, the outcasts, the foreigners, widows – the dis-membered ones. Jesus points to this poor, unnamed widow as an example of someone who is nearer the kingdom of God than the self-righteous scribes. And in doing this Jesus restores the balance, restores justice, casting off the unjust, the powerful. Jesus brings healing and hope, Jesus re-members the dis-membered ones.

This is a day of remembrance

And we remember that Jesus came to show us how much God loves the world. All of the world, even the unlovely bits. Especially the unlovely bits. So we must turn again to the world and celebrate God's good news about being members of one human race. We have to re-member . . . for re-membering can bring healing and hope. And we have to begin with ourselves, begin by allowing ourselves to be healed, to be put-back-together. It involves allowing ourselves to remember the pain of the past in order to begin to let go and commit to living in the present, it involves allowing ourselves to dream of the future.

But we do not stand alone in our brokenness. We are part of this local community in all its brokenness and pain. We are called to re-member this community with its poverty, crime, racism, drug abuse, apathy and depression. But we are also called to remember its vibrant life, its individuals, community events, residents' associations, to remember that there is much we can be proud of.

To re-member is to begin to heal our community, to stand up against racism and injustice, to work together to reduce crime, to be involved in the regeneration process, to bring justice and reconciliation between neighbours.

To re-member is to reach out from our own brokenness to embrace the brokenness of our wider world. To remember that we are all part of a bigger picture, that we do have a voice, that we can work towards a wider vision of justice and peace that recognizes that all people together make up this one dis-membered, divided world.

And as Christians we must also remember that we are part of Christ's broken but also resurrected body, that we are called to share in God's work of reconciling, of loving and healing in our dis-membered world.

This is a day of remembrance

And each time we share an act of remembrance, we are moving closer towards God's vision of justice, peace and hope, God's shalom.

Clare McBeath
England

95

Re-member the Future
Written on Holocaust Memorial Day

Remember past killings
with sorrow and shame
and make sure the present
has none of the same;
and work for a future
released from the past
when murderous madness
won't linger or last.

Preventing the hatreds
is all that now counts . . .
but these are our death-times,
the slaughtering mounts;
as we now have the will
we have long had the means:
the machetes and missiles
and killing machines.

Well-learnt is the language
of vengeance and war
that denounces evil
by creating more;
so well does it profit
to stir up alarms
to maintain the profits
of rough trade in arms.

With healing non-violence
less practised than preached
the best aims of the past
have still to be reached;
the worst stays to haunt us
so with no surprise

we look to the future
with fear in our eyes.

Take one of the hard men,
look him straight in the eye,
explain all the reasons
why no others need die;
in view of shared dangers
ask him to be willing
to help start the process
that stops all the killing.

David J. Harding
England

Inside Out

Black, white and gold
Are the colours of life –

For sorrow is black;
And the small seed of kindness
Unseen:
And the velvet of night
That hides love . . .

And the colour of skin.

For whiteness is pure,
And the breathless potential
Of dawn
Is revealed in the light
That hides nothing . . .

And the colour of skin.

For gold is of joy;
And the shining of sunlight
Unspent;
And the heat of the fire
That heals all . . .

And the colour of skin.

If the colours of life
Are the colours of skin –
Which clothes and encloses
The essence within –

Then the blood and the tears
Are the same.

Margot Arthurton
England

Black and White

black and white – I saw it in black and white
and it was signed in blood
kinship and sacrifice
the covenant
that binds us all together
in God's love

and I knew that black and white together
sealed with red
make all things one

the colours fuse
with sunlight
moonlight, starlight,
lovelight

to brown and pink and gold
in God's
kaleidoscope of life
and love

but we
confused
idolize one colour
our colour
black or white
the best
the only colour

and the kaleidoscope is broken
and the covenant
lies trampled in the dark
black and white
and red
with the blood of the victim

Heather Pencavel
England

House of Bread

The light of God has come into this world
To the House of Bread – given for the world
It started in Bethlehem – broken for all
Bethlehem – House of Bread

Womb of our hope, let all people be fed
As we share bread in the House of Bread
From our neighbours in the mosque next door –
                              I hear the call to prayer
As a candle of hope is lit in the House of Bread

Eating bread together means . . . eternal bonds
of love and friendship
In Bethlehem, where God visited our world
We still hear God through echoes of the angel's songs
And our high calling is still to give glory to God
and still to be peacemakers

In the House of Bread the Spirit of the living God rejuvenates us
To work in love
for peace with justice . . .
And never to despair

In the House of Bread the Spirit of the living God
Has refreshed us to commit ourselves to each other
In joy and pain
To work for healing and reconciliation

In the House of Bread broken for all
The Spirit of the living God has renewed us
God has become our liberator – our Sabeel –
our way and our living water

The light of God has come into this world
To the House of Bread – given for the world
It started in Bethlehem – broken for all
Bethlehem – House of Bread

Garth Hewitt
St Catherine's Church, Bethlehem

Speak to My Silence

Come, oh come little bird of peace.

Midwife of creation, source of life and wholeness, painter of the
rainbow, depth of well-being. You bring the calm, you tame the
storm, you soothe my fright and still my heart.

In place of fear you weave harmony; in place of discord you distribute good will.

Yet you come only when invited, you appear only when sought.

Unbidden, you are hidden; concealed in green nature but glimpsed in the leaf flicker; down in deep water but spied in the ripple; lost in the azure dome, yet reflected in sunlight.

Still, small voice, speak to my silence, reign in my soul and let me sing for you.

Judy Gunthorpe
England

Prayer for Life

Creator God, we come to you in prayer,
We come to you subdued by the events happening in the
   world today.
How often have we cried to You that our eyes may be opened,
   Our eyes!
How often have we cried to You that our mouths may speak
   words of love,
Not condemnation, *Our* mouths!
Almighty Teacher, teach us other ways of seeing,
Other ways of hearing,
Teach us a new language, the language of Jesus Christ
And lead us towards a new understanding of our fellow
   human beings
That touched by your love, barriers **can** be broken
And the reality of peace will come.
Amen.

Pamela Klimcke
Ireland

Envisioning Peace

The cries of war
drown out the pleas for forgiveness.
God, give us your wisdom.

The dreams of new life
lie dying in a mother's arms.
God, give us your hope.

The money needed to educate and feed
is used to buy weapons to kill.
God, give us your peace.

If we follow your call,
will you lead us to your peace?
If we embrace that peace,
will you provide for our needs?
If we trust your provision,
will you free us to see your face
in everyone we meet?

For when the guns are quiet,
we can hear one another.
When we are not busy with war,
we can feed a hungry child.
And when we envision your peace,
we cannot live any other way.

Louise Margaret Granahan
Canada

Convert Weapons into Goods

Now is the time, as ever is,
for us to transcend history,
converting weapons into goods,
fulfilling ancient prophecy.

Disarm the man, disarm the state
to find the new security
of living without lethal threat
and handling conflict properly.

We pray for those responsible
for finding and developing
new ways and means to safeguard peace
and peaceful ways of managing.

So may the dividends of peace
be shared with care so all maintain
their proper right to livelihood
and never yearn for war again.

Harness our passions, calm our fears
and sublimate our energies
so we can mobilize ourselves
to be friends to our enemies.

David J. Harding
England

Weapons of War
Hosea 2:18

God promised us peace. All strife would cease.
All weapons of war would go from the land.
Swords were among those. He spoke of bows.
Such envoys of death are held in the hand.

But what of the mind? What do we find?
Which weapons of war exist in the head?
But, even more so, how can we know
How heart of soul can pile up the dead?

Ah, never did steel hatefulness feel;
Nor iron agree to launch an onslaught.
But envy can lead, combined with greed,
To a reservoir of murderous thought.

For lust for power turns motives sour,
With selfish clinching the will to kill;
And malice can bring a wicked thing,
Sick ruthlessness wanting much blood to spill.

Healing must begin right from within
If he who's a hawk can yet be a dove.
See whether our heart can play its part,
By trying to act like the King of love.

'Bless your enemy', He says to me.
'And to violence turn the other cheek.'
For happy are they who are and pray
That peace will transcend the conflict so bleak.

Alan Hiscock
England

Swords into Ploughshares

'I came not to bring peace but a sword.'
Why did you have to say that, O Lord?
Didn't you realize how it could be used against you?
And against us?
Couldn't you have stuck to healing people
And preaching the good news?

We watched the news today.
So much hurt; so much suffering.
Help us to see others
As you see each of us.
Give us a vision
And a faith that the vision may be realized.

We ask this, hoping that salvation is closer now than when we
   first believed.
Amen.

Michael Reiss
England

A New Kind of War

'Everything is in place
on the humanitarian front
and on the military front,'
said the Prime Minister.
Amen:

we want it to be different this time.

New cruise missiles
are in the air with warheads of love,
so even the ones that miss
will cause collateral healing, that's how much

we want it to be different this time.

Our armies will move into Al Qaeda towns
with cranes and concrete mixers,
resurrect the building firms,
and coax people back home again, to show

we want it to be different this time.

The SAS will go in dancing,
the Marines will start cricket teams,
the suicide bombers will start to smile, we're serious,

we want it to be different this time.

We've organized giant earth movers
to excavate huge reservoirs, to drain
thousands of years,
Jerusalems of tears, oh how much

we want it to be different this time.

It's been thousands of years,
Jerusalems of tears,

and we want it to be different this time.

Geoffrey Herbert
England

Retaliate with Peace

We who
would not 'play with fire'
must keep our distance from
those nukey little bully-boys
who burn down towns
just to smoke out
the naughty tantrum-troubled
'box of matches'
silly baby arsonists.

Then
distanced from the deeds
we must keep close enough,
with more than fingers burnt,
to Peace
warmed hearts aflame
with all-converting Love

for those sad few
who 'know not what they do'
when
glibly getting rid of some
in some fine cause
to spite them all

but even more
for those bad many
powerful rich
whose lame response
is
to get rid of all
to rid themselves of some
destroying the destroyers
by
destroying everything.

David J. Harding
England

Cold Waters Flood Across the Ground

Cold waters flood across the ground;
The clouds shut out the sun.
Torrential rain stings all around,
The darkness has begun.
No stir of any living breath
Is found upon the earth
But, safe within the Ark of death,
Lies what God brings to birth.

The raven beats across the flood
But sees no place to stand.
The dove of peace now risks her blood
To find some friendly land.

The olive branch is seized at last;
The Ark lies on the shore.
The love of God has held us fast;
We are afraid no more.

Stephen Orchard
England

On the Road to Jericho

It was no five-minute miracle.
These things take time, you said,
and you sat beside me,
at the edge of the road,
your hands on my eyes,
slowly and gently removing
my judgemental attitudes.

I admit I felt vulnerable.
There's comfort in shadows.
The world of light was so vast
that if you hadn't been there,
I might have changed my mind,
but your touch spoke to my eyes
and there was no going back.

As you healed my blindness,
you asked me what I could see
but I didn't have words
to describe the loveliness
emerging from the light
or what that loveliness
was doing to my heart.

It was beauty, you said,
without the blindness of judgement.
The eyes see only beauty

and when the eyes see only beauty,
the heart knows only love.
The heart that knows only love,
you said, is in the presence of God.

I told you I couldn't see as well as that,
and you reminded me again
that miracles took time.

Joy Cowley
Aotearoa New Zealand

Trees and Flowers and Mountain Springs

Trees and flowers and mountain springs
praise the grace of God Creator,
in whose breathing birds can sing,
in whose love creation grows.
Scents of forests, dancing winds,
rain and sunshine, crystal snowflakes
bring their soundless joy to you,
God of life and truth.

You were born as a child of peace
and you walked the way of passion.
Love may grow and peace increase,
when we walk the way of Christ.
Every little newborn child,
man and woman, every heartbeat
bring their joy of life to you,
God of peace and truth.

Hear the sound of the blowing wind,
whispering our longing prayers.
Holy Spirit, come and bring
life and peace for times to come.

Listen, people sing new songs,
love is breathing, truth is winning.
Thus we lay our hope in you,
God of love and truth.

Per Harling
Sweden

Flowing Water

Water flows softly
with incoming tide;
long ago
it brought the Viking ships
to plunder, pillage and kill.
Now it brings touring yachts
to browse and buy.

Waters flow softly.
Where once rivers ran red
with the violence of war
now they stay clear
and mark refreshing peace.

Lord of the flowing water
grant us peace in our time.
May nations work together;
may hurts be healed;
may our children learn
the joy of mutual care.

John Johansen-Berg
England

A Psalm: Unity

*Behold, how good and how pleasant it is for brethren
to dwell together in unity.
(Psalm 133:1)

There is joy in concord for all people
When words say new what is seen fresh;
When voices sing songs to mend broken speech
And make sound whole;
When fragments, indifferent and abandoned,
Make an unheard harmony.

There is blessing in concord for all people
When the Lord anoints his high priest –
Counterpoint to holiness – with love.
He kneels, his prayers inflect
Supplications with freedom:
With suffering.

There is peace in concord for all people
When bread is shared, beggars embrace,
Donors repent and healing abounds.
For unity is a story attuned – in
Mysterious triple echoes – to
Love's glory.

Derek Webster
England

111

Be Free of the Shadows

May the road be free for the journey,
May it lead where it promised it would,
May the stars that gave ancient bearings
Be seen, and still be understood.

May the knife remain in the holder,
May the bullet stay in the gun,
May those who live in the shadows
Be seen by those in the sun.

Author Unknown
Australia

What Does It Take to Start a Fire?

What does it take to start a fire?

Fuel, a spark, and the intention to use them.

What does it take to start a fire?

The fuel of injustice piled upon injustice.
The fuel of atrocity and retaliation rehearsed for generations.
The fuel of hopes dashed, promises broken and cries ignored.

The spark of a minor incident that becomes an excuse.
The spark of a speech crafted to incite.
The spark of an act designed to provoke.

Brought together, spark and fuel can ignite an inferno.

So what does it take to quench the blaze, to snuff out the spark
    and dampen the fuel?

It takes the imagination to see that fear, sin and sorrow are not
the monopoly of just one side.
It takes the courage to speak and act for tolerance,
understanding and justice.
It takes the confidence to see that people and situations can be
retrieved from violence.
It takes the faith to trust that we can work for God in building
peace.

Neil Thorogood
England

Contemplation of a White Rose

White Rose God,
I delight in Your purity,
I seek Your sweet beauty;
I see that You are without peer,
Oh White Rose God, shining with dew-gentle tears
which gleam, highlighting
the outer petal sphere.
Such tears appear Divine, of Spirit Love
Sun-warmed by White Son Joy
Wing-wiped by Eternal Dove
As it coo-calls from within the throat of Peace.

And as You reveal yourself increasingly
So do we offer praise and admiration,
Praise and adulation
Most properly.
We delight in You, White Rose God
Your fragrance entices.
We reach for You.

Glenn Jetta Barclay
Aotearoa New Zealand

The Gift

God grant us the gift of dreaming:

The dream of a world enjoying its extraordinary colour and
    beauty –
  Not viewing life through tunnel-visioned, grey-tinted
    spectacles.
The dream of breadth and variety in glorious harmony –
  Not definition through division, prejudice and ignorance.
The dream of acceptance and inclusion –
  Not judgement and exclusion.
The dream of Your love and humour –
  Not our idolatry and self-righteousness.
The dream of 'we might' –
  Not 'we cannot'.

God give us the vision and imagination to dream
and enable us to make the dream a reality.
Amen.

Zam Walker
Wales/Scotland

Harmony

The basis of human relationship –
    of unity, understanding, fellowship –
is not that all should be as one
    (of one mind, one conviction,
    of one colour, creed or culture)
but that in our diversity
we should reach out our hands
and claim each other's difference
as enrichment of ourselves.

Human experience is not to be encapsulated
    in one place or time or race

but each individual brings
a grain of understanding
to place in the magnificent mosaic.

Thus God beholds his created work
not in shades of grey
but in the glorious colours
    of bright yellow cheerfulness
    and deep blue despair;
    green hope and growing things,
    brown security and earth;
    black treacly richness
    and the white of an empty page.

He sees no flatness in creation
but the high relief
    of mountains and valleys,
    ecstasy and doubt,
    barren wintry deserts
    and warm pastures.

The difficulties we find in our relationships
are often in our seeking to find
likeness between green and red,
compromise of sea and fire:

    It cannot be.

We must learn to stand apart,
to say: I am I and you are you –
    are we not beautiful?
    How great is our Creator.
    O make of our diversity
    something
    worth his dying for.

Elizabeth Mackey
England

115

God, Your Gift of Peace Is Precious

God, your gift of peace is precious
In this world of sin and loss:
You have given joy and gladness,
Making peace through Jesus' cross.
God, in love you came to save us,
Giving freedom from our sin –
In you, gifts of peace begin.

Jesus, you are God's example
In the life on earth you lived.
Help us see your face in others,
Teach us freely to forgive.
When, in all your children's conflicts,
Hate and violence increase –
Blest are those who work for peace.

Blessed are the poor in spirit;
Blessed, too, are all the meek.
When we feel a slap of hatred,
You say: Turn the other cheek.
When arrested in the garden
You spoke to your friend to say,
'Peter, put your sword away.'

Spirit, help us work for justice
In each challenge that we face.
Each one needs to have the other:
Righteousness and peace embrace.
Children hungry? People homeless?
Missiles flying through the air?
You seek peace with justice there.

So we pray and work together
Toward a world of your shalom.
May all people share your bounty,

And all have both feast and home.
Wolf and lamb shall feed together:
In your kingdom war shall cease,
And your people live in peace.

Tune: Cwm Rhondda

Carolyn Winfrey Gillette
USA

I Am Because We Are

we are children of a common culture
sharing visions, dreams and ways of seeing
affirming one another as we speak
a common language
I am because we are

we are citizens of one country
bound in a common economic system
and I work too long and spend my waking hours
stressed and exhausted, overwhelmed, while you,
you have no work at all, no sense of worth,
long empty days to spend alone
I am because we are

we are dwellers in one city
walk the same streets in the same sun and rain
and I go home to comfort and good food
to lights and known voices, and a private place
while you take shelter in shop doorways, beg for coins,
sleep under bridges, eat rubbish from the bins
and fear the darkness and the stranger's voice
I am because we are

we are people of one world
sharing resources, needing each other's work
and I destroy you when I consume

unwittingly, and waste and spoil,
tear down the trees, pollute the patient earth
and I am rich and you are poor
I am because we are

we are children of one God
made in God's image, needing God's kin(g)dom
of just love (*just* love?) for our redemption
God says
I AM – therefore you are
my kin(g)dom is among you now
do you not know?
I am the person standing next to you
your kin
your king

Heather Pencavel
England

A Peace Blessing

Living, Loving God, Creator of Humankind,
Bless each one of us as we go on our way,
individually or together,
with love and unity of purpose.

Loving Christ, Creator of Compassion,
Bless us as we strive to bring compassion
into the search for global peace;
Bless us in our efforts to influence leaders
and politicians.

Refreshing, Dancing Spirit, Creator of Vitality,
Bless and encourage us to engage in lively activity
for peace and justice
in global situations;

to turn disappointments into challenges,
to transform darkness into light,
to root God-given,
Christ-like ideals wherever we and other people walk.

Geoffrey Duncan
England

Chapter Four
Where There Is No Peace

Words for Peace

In the heat of memory we recall
that for every victory
there is a loss;
that for every ceasefire
there is a sniper;
that for every liberation
there is a prison;
that for every peace agreement
there is a continued conflict;
if not above our skies,
if not in our waters,
if not in these islands,
if not on our doorstep,
then in some forgotten field.
We will remember them.

Janet Lees
England

Blood Brothers

A song sparked off by the book Blood Brothers *by Elias Chacour*

When will the children of Abraham find their peace?
When will the children of Abraham find their peace?
When will the children of Abraham find their peace?
When will the children of Abraham find their peace?

Blood brothers, who've shared the same grief –
Homes taken, being refugees.
Blood brothers, who've shared the same fear –
The midnight knock and the soldiers there,
The soldiers there – it's a constant fear.

When will the children . . .

Blood brothers with the same plea:
'Give us land where we can be free.'

Blood brothers, with a wounded past,
How long must your sorrow last –
Will it last – must it last?

Does it have to be this way?
Does it have to be this way?
Soldier, throw that gun away.
From Galilee came a man,
He shed His blood upon this land,
Pouring peace from wounded hands.

When will the children . . .

Blood brothers, in the same land;
With the same father – Abraham,
You are Jew and Palestinian;
Will you ever walk hand in hand –
Hand in hand make a Holy Land?

Does it have to be this way?
Does it have to be this way?
Soldier, throw that gun away.
From Galilee came a man,
He shed His blood upon this land,
Pouring peace from wounded hands.

When will the children . . .

Garth Hewitt
England

Where There Is No Peace (1)
Written for the people who share in my struggle

The dispossession of black people from land in South Africa
initially took place at the hands of white colonizers, and
through legislation.

Black people were forced off their land and made to resettle.

Under apartheid an estimated 3.5 million people were removed from rural and urban areas to where there were no infrastructures or other services.

My reflection is from my own experience and I suppose many black South Africans can identify with these feelings.

Land! Land! Where is my Father's land?
Fertile soil! Where is my Father's fertile soil?
Awake!
The noise of bulldozers fills the air, dust and tears mingle
   down my face.
'Gee pad hotnot' (out of the way Koi Khoi).
Our land, fertile soil,
Our source of income has vanished.

Who are you?
Who has given you the right?
Where are you from?
'Dad! Dad! Who are they?
Show yourselves to me!' Screamed the grade six kid.
White, yet faceless, they are;
Frustrated and angry, I am.

Peace! Peace! Lasting peace, pleads the new South Africa.
Peace, I said,
What kind of peace?

I am hurting –
The pain in my heart,
The pain in my soul.
What about confession?
What about forgiveness?
What about restitution?
What about reconciliation?

Who has messed up this process?
The pain, the hurt –

Who has messed up my emotions?
Is it you, Desmond Tutu?
Is it you, Nelson Mandela?
Lord, Lord is it you?

Oh my Lord, this peace, this unnatural peace. You demand
 from me.
I sometimes feel your demand is simply too high.

Is it all right to feel like this?
Where there is no peace . . .
There is hatred . . . there is violence . . . there is bloodshed.

More than twenty years later I can only utter these prayers:
'Oh God, help me in my efforts to work for lasting peace.'
   I have chaired many Truth and Reconciliation meetings in
Johannesburg, always with the struggle deep inside of me –
'Am I doing the right thing?'

Why Am I Here?

Why am I here?
Look – and look again.
What do you see?
Black people – Yes, black people.
One . . . two . . . three . . . four white faces,
Three young people – one aged person.
Where are the other white people?
They are not here.

Who will listen to my story?
Who will listen to what I have to say?
Or shall we only heal our own memories?
Healing of memories! Yes, healing of memories.

Where are you white folk?
Come out of your comfort zones,

Listen to us, listen to what I have to say.
Take my hand
Let's walk together
Let's reconcile
Let's build
Let's work for peace.

Kelvin Harris
South Africa

Do Not Say 'Peace'

Lord, let us not say 'peace'
where there is no peace,
where children have gnawing hunger,
where rural people are exploited,
where city dwellers are crowded into slums,
where those who speak for freedom are tortured.
Deliver us from saying 'peace'
where there is injustice.
Lead us into word and action
that challenge oppression
and call for true peace, your peace.

John Johansen-Berg
England

I Cannot Live As If Peace Is of No Importance

Lord of our motivation
encourage us to keep going,
enable us to be ever more
determined to work for what
we believe
might be . . .
Peace.

All: I cannot live as if Peace is of no importance.

When we see people on a television screen:

the women
  the men
    the children
injured
  distraught
    bereaved
all certainly traumatized . . .

They are flesh and blood . . .
with human feelings . . .
suffering . . .
according to the ways
and understandings in which they live their lives.

All: I cannot live as if Peace is of no importance.

Thank you for the investigative journalists
the television reporters
the women and men who put their lives on the line . . .
so that we might see and have some knowledge . . .
and try to understand . . .
Thank you to the Holy One who seeks to protect them

All: I cannot live as if Peace is of no importance.

Geoffrey Duncan
England

Peace Is Fragile

The 'hill of crosses' is a place of pilgrimage for the people of
Lithuania. A modest hill out in the countryside, it is a potent
reminder of a remorseless totalitarian past; many died in those
heartless and inhumane days. Peace is more fragile than we often
realize. The cross is an eternal reminder to us of that fragility.

Stephen Platten
England

What Is Peace?

At a Sudanese International Conference held in The Netherlands, 'Peace was identified as a shared vision and a necessary force to join hands, pick up the pieces and weave them together.'

Rebecca Joshua Okwaci is a Sudanese woman who has been working for peace and she has embarked on large scale peace-making in her war-torn country. She believes that more skills will enhance her capacity and enable her to contribute more effectively to the peace process. This process is not an easy task as the country has been ravaged by a four-decade-long war. The war has killed, maimed and uprooted citizens and rendered them internally displaced persons or refugees in neighbouring countries. Some activities in terms of sensitization on the meaning and need for peace, training on mediation and advocacy are just part of the aim of building a culture of tolerance, dialogue and eventually realizing peace.

Rebecca Joshua Okwaci
Sudan

Praying for Peace in Mozambique

More than eighty people were massacred in a police cell in Mozambique.

In the light of violence and conflicts that have become the order of the day in Mozambique, the Catholic bishops called for calm, condemning violence, regardless of where it came from.

'We renew vehemently the denunciation, the repudiation and implacable condemnation to the authors of death and other violations of human rights in general, especially to those responsible for the massacre and whose cruelty has never been witnessed in the history of our country.'

The Catholic Bishops
Episcopal Conference of Mozambique

Come Afresh on Your Holy Land

Heavenly Father,
In the life and ministry of your Son, Jesus Christ, you showed
  us how to live together;
give this sense of unity to the peoples of the Holy Land today.
In the death of your Son on the Cross,
you showed how great was your love for us as well as your
  readiness to forgive;
you brought new hope to your people and a desire to work for
  peace and justice;
renew that hope in your people today
and give them a burning desire to find your peace in this time.
In the resurrection of Jesus and in the outpouring of your
  Holy Spirit
you showed the disciples they had power and authority to
  conquer in your name;
convince your people today of the gifts you have entrusted to
  them
and so help them to transform their Land to your greater
  glory.
We ask this in Jesus' name.
Amen.

His Grace Bishop Riah Abu El-Assal
Jerusalem

Spirit of the Living God

Spirit of the Living God,
Come afresh on your Holy Land.
Help your people to restore broken relationships.
Give them patience to break down barriers of suspicion and
  mistrust;
ability to discern personal prejudice and the courage to
  overcome fear.

Encourage them to respect each other's integrity and rights
so that your kingdom may be established on earth for Jesus'
   sake.
Amen.

His Grace Bishop Riah Abu El-Assal
Jerusalem

We Searched for Peace

We searched for peace on planet earth
but it was difficult to find.
In Latin America people still suffered
from the after-effects of oppression.
In Africa there was a bitter legacy
from the days of colonialism.
In Europe the clouds of two world wars
hung heavy in the evening air.
So we journeyed to the holy land,
guided by a star, and came at last to Bethlehem.
There were tanks waiting on the village streets
and children with stones in their hands
and tears in their eyes.
Would that planet earth
knew the things that make for peace.
Return, Jesus, redeemer and saviour,
and show us how to find the blessing of peace.

John Johansen-Berg
Engand

The African Child's Cry

Mother, where are you?
Father, I do not see you.
I am so afraid of the dark,

Even though the dogs do not bark.
What am I to do now,
There is no one left in the town?

You told me to run and hide,
I took your word, trusting like a child.
For a long while I heard loud noises,
Then, all of a sudden complete silence.
I crept out of my hiding place,
And looked around me – what a mess!

I cannot understand why
Hands, legs, bodies just lie
About scattered, everywhere.
I ran to our house, it was nowhere
To be seen. Mother, can you hear me?
I am so hungry.
Help me up father, I am weak and thirsty.

The Gambia Unit
World Federation of Methodist
and Uniting Church Women

How Can I See a Single Face

A reflection on the difficulty of visualizing an individual on hearing of
2 million deaths in war in Africa – Congo and Rwanda – in two years

How can I see a single face
amid this madding throng,
this mass of human misery,
all prey to human wrong?

How can I grasp a reaching hand
where thousands blur as one
within this taut cacophony
beneath this searing sun?

Show me a single pleading face,
offer an open hand,
help me to grasp the evidence
that I might understand.

Give me an openness of heart,
a willingness of mind
to meet the stark necessity
of crying humankind.

Give me a surfeit of the love
that gave creation birth,
that I might see within this throng
each individual's worth.

Andrew Pratt
England

O God, Our Words Cannot Express

This hymn was written on 11 September 2001 whilst watching the news reports about terrorist attacks in New York City, Pennsylvania and Washington DC. It was shared on the internet and used by many congregations as well as on national US television and the UK BBC. The hymn is timeless and may well be used in times of strife and war.

O God, our words cannot express
The pain we feel this day.
Enraged, uncertain, we confess
Our need to bow and pray.

We grieve for all who lost their lives
And for each injured one.
We pray for children, husbands, wives,
Whose grief has just begun.

O Lord, we're called to offer prayer
For all our leaders, too.
May they, amid such great despair,
Be wise in all they do.

We trust your mercy and your grace;
In you we will not fear!
May peace and justice now embrace!
Be with your people here!

Tune: St Anne

Carolyn Winfrey Gillette
USA

Prodigal Father

Twin towers
Collapse.

New York, 2001

In less than an hour,
The world is blown apart
By a huge unthinkable act
Of terror,
Evil, deadly terror.

Lost for words,
We stand and stare at the images before our eyes.
Our world,
Your world,
For ever changed.

We know you teach that weeds will grow
Amongst the wheat,
And evil coexist with good,

Rise up to counteract and choke . . .
But, this much Lord?
No, surely not.
This is much more,
Much more than we can bear.

Your world, your people
Need you Lord.
We need you now
As never before:
Not passive, distant comforter,
No, more than that
We need you here
Alive, pro-active in our pain.

Running to meet us,
Matching the speed of those who run in fear.

We need our prodigal Father
Now.

Prayer seems inadequate today.
We can't make sense of this.
Yet pray we must.

And so we ask,
We ask you Lord
With greater fervour than we've ever known
That you will use
This tide of questioning, this sea of pain,
To fuel
A great outpouring of your love,

A love so big
That it can heal
And change;

Can help the wheat grow tall,
Grow strong,
And rise above
The deadly weeds.

Pat Marsh
England

Destruction and Violence
Written in response to the events of 11 September 2001

I looked at the world of destruction
and violence to people on earth,
I cried out to God, 'Will you save us?
Can justice and peace come to birth?'
    'Go up,' said God, 'to the watch-tower
    and look for the vision of life.
    It hastens, though you feel it tarries.
    The nations shall overcome strife.'

I saw the remains of earth's bombsite,
the hunger and carnage of war.
I cried out to God, 'What is happening?
What have you created us for?'
    'Go up,' said the Lord, 'and keep watching.
    The God of all people shall prove
    To be faithful to ALL people
    As ALL shall be safe in my love.'

I saw people, greed and oppression,
the terror, the bloodshed, the hate,
I cried out to God, 'God, where are you?
Have you left your poor world to its fate?'
    'Rise up,' said the Lord, 'I am with you.
    I have shared in the world's and your pains.

God of Christian, of Jew and of Muslim
One God, ever faithful remains.'

David Fox
Wales

Tuesday

Clear blue skies
Two towers – reflecting glass
    gleaming concrete
Below the canyons – side-walk bustle
      security in the humdrum
Another day, another dollar.

Clear blue skies
Two planes – shining metal
    thundering power
Travellers – dozing? unexpecting?
Safe in the ordinariness, the limbo of travel.

BUT . . . watching
  waiting
    grasping the moment
      denying fear, brave to the death, self-justified.

AND THEN
Grey, brown skies – swirling, dust laden
    shattered glass
     dulled crumbled concrete
Rubble-packed canyons – bodies, broken
Not 'another' day but 'the' day.

The day security, the humdrum, the ordinary –
    disappeared.

In the silence of the aftershock, the world prays.

Ann Coates
England

New York 11/9/01

High, high they rose
Thrust to the sky
Shining in mirrored mimicry –
Bright twins
And proud of it;

Then from that sky
Came death
And shattering
Of mirror images – and lives.

And all the thrust
Of plans and powers
Sank with the sigh
Of prisoned souls
To dust . . .

And the dust rose up
And thrust
Into the eyes of God

And God wept.

Margot Arthurton
England

Last Holiday Season
The Holiday Season can be the part of the year which is relevant to a
culture and/or celebration

Last holiday season we were placing wreaths on the doors of
   our homes;
this holiday season many are placing wreaths on the graves of
   our heroes.

Last holiday season many were letting their sons play with
toy guns;
this holiday season they are teaching them that guns are not
toys.

Last holiday season we were counting our money;
this holiday season we are counting our blessings.

Last holiday season we were lighting candles to decorate;
this holiday season we are lighting candles to commemorate.

Last holiday season we were thinking about all the things we
didn't have;
this holiday season we are thinking about all the things we do
have.

Last holiday season we were thinking about the madness of
holidays;
this holiday season we are thinking about the meaning of them.

Last holiday season we were giving thanks for gifts from stores;
this holiday season we are giving thanks for gifts from God.

Last holiday season we were wondering how to give our
children all the things that money can buy – the hottest toys,
the latest fashions, the newest gadgets;
this holiday season we are wondering how to give them all
the things we can't – a sense of security, safety, peace.

Last holiday season we were thinking about how good it
would feel to be affluent;
this holiday season we are thinking how good it feels to be
alive.

Last holiday season we thought angels were in heaven;
this holiday season we know some are right here on earth.

Last holiday season 'peace on earth' is something we prayed
    for on Sunday mornings;
now it is something we pray for every day.

Anonymous

There Is God and All of God Is There

The horrors of our history are vast, beyond belief.
We greet each new atrocity with bafflement, or grief,
yet all the evil energies that haunt the human race
come, not from alien galaxies, but from our inner space,
    and terror, pain and genocide intrude on every prayer,
    with shades that whisper, 'Where is God? If only God were there!'

By torture, war and poverty, by flame and firing squad,
for glory, flag and destiny, and with a prayer to God,
God's image finds a thousand ways to torment, and to kill,
and asks how love can justify such terrible free will:
    for every cry of suffering will drive us back to prayer,
    as thousands clamour, 'Where is God? If only God were there!'

Yet, if like some robotic race, though warm with flesh and
    blood,
our happy self, with smiling face, was programmed to be
    good,
and had no freedom, seeing wrong, to seek it, or say no,
our praise would be a puppet-song and love, an empty show.
    Our pain and terror mark the cost of every faithful prayer
    that chooses justice, love and trust and hopes that God is there.

And God is not an analyst, observing gain and loss
but loves us to the uttermost and suffers on a cross:
for love comes, not like Heads of State, in power and glamour
    known,
but as a loser, desolate, in anguish and alone:

140

The cross, revealed in Easter light, will nourish every prayer
When faith discovers, 'There is God, and all of God is there!'

Brian Wren
England/USA

I Can't . . .

I'd like to stop
the manic rush to war . . .

                                   I can't!

I'd like to intercept
the bullets and the bombs . . .

                                   I can't!

I'd like to block
the flow of hate . . .

                                   I can't!

I'd like to quench
the flow of victim's blood . . .

                                   I can't!

I'd like to wave
a magic healing wand . . .

                                   I can't!

I'd like to change
the vengeful mind-sets of the hurt . . .

                                   I can't!

I'd like to sanitize
the madman's mind . . .

                                   I can't!

I'd like to convert
all warriors to peace . . .

                              I can't!

I'd like to turn around
the backward warmongers . . .

                              I can't!

I'd like to end
the bloodshed and the spite . . .

                              I can't!

I'd like to put
the so-wronged world to right . . .

                              I can't!

I can denounce, renounce
all war and violence . . .
just 'die to it' . . .
then,
resurrected into love
I can belong
to quite another way
whose truth and life
is to come some day
to come some day!

David J. Harding
England

Jesus in the Blackness

We are called to trust our God despite circumstances,
Jesus is not affected by the blackness we experience –
He is there, the same as always.
His power is the same,
His love is the same,

His forgiveness is the same,
His confidence and calm reassurance
Are the same.
He still believes in me,
He is not dismayed –
Neither should I be.

'Trust me, even in the blackness,' says Jesus,
As his light, power and love flow constantly and reliably
Making the blackness (even though it is still there)
Not quite so daunting.

The fear is gone,
The feeling of being overwhelmed by it
Is gone . . .
And Jesus' presence is discerned.

Ruth Sermon
England

No Angel Song

Those shepherds long ago
heard angels sing –
or so I'm told –
sense-tingling, mind-blowing
songs from outer space
filling the inner ear.
I strain my senses
but detect no sound
save that of shrivelled infants
sucking at empty breasts;
I see no visions,
only children blank-eyed
from mindless horrors.
O angels, sing again for me,
flood my night sky with your light.

My heart is raw with grief
for young men aged by pain,
girls twisted by abuse,
numbed by neglect.
Tear-blinded I go astray
and stumble in the dark.

No singing, then? No angels?
Only an olive grove and bloody sweat;
only a cross, but empty.
Lord help me where faith falters
and vision fades
and angels never sing.

Helene McLeod
England

Prayers for A Hurting World
*A chant from Taizé or the Iona Community could be used during
these intercessions*

Chant

We pray for people around our world
caught up in situations of conflict and violence
or suffering from famine or disaster.
We are embodied with them now.

Chant

We pray for the people and communities of faith
from whom we have come
and to whom we shall return.
We are embodied with them now.

Chant

We pray for those who are sick,
those who are bereaved or oppressed,
and those who are homeless.
We are embodied with them now.

Chant

We pray for the broken
and torn fabric of the earth
as it yearns for healing.
We are embodied with Christ in creation now.

Chant

And because you are one with us, O Christ,
enable us to share your life with the world by
sharing our own lives with the world
so we may live together in harmony and peace.

Chant

Clare McBeath
England

Spirit of Truth and Judgement

Spirit of truth and judgement,
Who alone can cast out the powers that grip our world,
At the point of crisis, give us your discernment,
That we may accurately name what is evil and know the way
     that leads to peace.
Through Jesus Christ our Lord.
Amen.

Roger Grainger
England

Dare I Pray?

Dare I pray for places of tension and hostility? The trip-off-the-tongue-prayer is so easy! God fix it, God fix *them*!

I pray for reconciliation in Northern Ireland, for the people of the Holy Land to live with one another in harmony and, yes, I pray for understanding between the races on these islands when I hear of tension or racial violence.

I pray quite often that *they* should learn to live with one another. That's right, isn't it, Lord!

Should I pray like this for peace and understanding, for reconciliation and greater understanding? Naturally I should. And yet, what about me, what about those prejudices I keep harboured within me and that I don't like others challenging?

Can I pray for *them* to live together when I stand aside from people because *they* are not able-bodied, or because *they* are not of my intelligence or because *they* are not of my gender or my sexual orientation?

To be honest, Lord, there are feelings in me, deep feelings, long-ago-learnt-feelings, feelings that, sometimes, I know I shouldn't have, just like feelings in Northern Ireland, in the Holy Land and in the racial kaleidoscope of these islands.

Dare I pray for peace and reconciliation amongst *them*? If I dare, then I'm giving you permission to change me, too. If *they* are to live together, then I must risk knowing, respecting, embracing and accepting as gifts from you, generous God, the *them* of my small mind and heart.

John Ll. Humphreys
Scotland/Wales

Naboth and the Unnamed Woman
A meditation based upon 1 Kings 21 and Mark 14:3–9

Remember me, a man of no real importance,
though you may know my name.
Do not let my stand and my sacrifice
be forever ignored.
Stand alongside me in your world today:

in Palestine, Israel and the West Bank,
where unknown, innocent victims
are maimed and killed
in fighting over land.

Stand alongside me in urging your leaders
to continue the struggle for a just and equitable settlement
to such troubles, a fair and lasting peace.

Stand alongside me when peace missions and summit
meetings fail:
to stop the fighting,
to care for God's creation,
to steward its resources responsibly for future generations,
to stop the emission of toxic waste,
to prevent the destruction of rain forests,
to stem the tide of pollution that poisons your rivers and seas.

Stand alongside me in your willingness to pay a fair price
for the products you consume,
so that small farmers and local co-operatives
can live off their land with security and peace of mind.

For I am Naboth and my blood still cries out to be heard.

Remember me, a woman of no importance,
belittled, dismissed, unnamed.
Do not let my faith and my action be forever ignored.

Stand alongside me and honour me in your world today,
as I recognized and honoured Christ,
as he received and respected me.

Stand alongside me in every place
of sacrifice and suffering,
where unnamed women weep for husbands and children
whose bodies cannot be anointed for burial
because they have been blown to bits;
where unnamed women join hands in shared sorrow
across racial, religious and political divides,
to draw wounded and broken communities together,
to be prophets of peace.

For though my name is unknown,
still my sorrow and my sacrifice
cry out to be heard.

God of justice, peace and love,
we offer our prayers for all
whose needs we have called to mind
through the story of Naboth
and the unnamed woman.
Do not let us be content
to let the matter end here.
Show us, through them,
how to look at ourselves,
our values and beliefs,
our personal priorities and plans,
and those of the governments
we place in power,
through your eyes.
Teach us through them
to turn our prayers
into committed actions.

Jean Mortimer
England

Messiah Journey

I am the man who boarded the cattle truck
and was counted by a clerk.
I am the clerk.
I am the woman you hear inside wailing
for her dead boy
still wearing his royal star of David.
I am the child.

I am the farmer watching his furrow
and the businessman looking intently for another train
and I am the driver in the sidings
shunting the blind containers,
knowing what is in them, and hurrying
to catch the tram homewards.

I am the gaping gateway at the halt,
whose mouth speaks of making people free,
then grabs them, shuts and swallows.
I am the grey men and their grey dogs.
I am the ice-cold stripping-place
and the steel door at the other end.
I am the Zyclon powder from above.
I am the howling and the gnashing of teeth,
the absolute despair of love,
the naked clutching arms,
the silence after psalms.

Geoffrey Herbert
England

Sarajevo

Dimming light hems me around. Crushed, after days
Of limb-locked struggle, winter enemies brace
Me to time's wall, to unmake my making.

149

Breath thins to anguish, pain in focus;
Dreams are shredded, faith turns to unrhyming dogma.
I am among the dead who colonize the edge of night
And receive no lodging in tomorrow's hope.

Kin to corpses, naked and grimed for the grave,
I hang unseen in an emptiness without guests,
Pinned to lime-washed walls, round round walls.
Such hurt remains love's question.

Death and its implicit acolyte, unpaid pain, strip my life.
Reliable phantoms scourge, red-swaddle me in flames.
Skin has no reprieve from their ripening plagues.
In this tight fear my tenancy of life nears its close.

Principals in an arena of cruelty, they twist pain to
Torment, define me for the stress of death. Scars multiply.
No gloss of ease deadens their clasp. Agony patents my life.
I have come to the place where suffering is conceived.

The brilliant nightmare is real, time is torn, the future
Has fled, beauty is effaced in a monotony of dust. I see
Daisy suns no more, nor fly with herons to wind marshes.
Death's dark crawls closer each hour.

Pain swells to an unbearable rack. That I am, brings
Their sharpest condemnation. Now, exiled, transfigured to
Night, in ashes of slashed lemon wood, they show me
The withered eyes of children – my child – lining trim graves.

Shall I adjourn the task of words? Can such a psalm be
    spoken?
Should talk inflect horror, give it symmetry, proportion and
    rhythm?
Yet not to speak poisons words and fractures the world. So
    speak . . .

Derek Webster
England

150

Goodness is Stronger than the Evil

Goodness is stronger than the evil.
Love bears, believes and hopes all things.
Light sees through the deepest darkness.
Truth lives where the freedom sings.

Power is made perfect in the weakness.
Justice will open doors of fear.
Courage roots in true compassion,
Gives to hope the power to spear.

Per Harling
Sweden

Peace – Like a Phoenix

From the ashes of yesterday's dreams, we long to see you rise
Wipe the tears away from your eyes
Oh the bitterness that salts your wounds, let it wash away
Let's hear you say, let's hear you say,

Let peace like a phoenix rise again
Let tears of forgiveness fall like rain
Let there be a new breath in the valley of death
Let peace like a phoenix rise again.

With your hand wipe away the hatred we see
Father of all, set us free
With the sword that sheds no blood, break the pride and let
there bud
A tree of life, a tree of life,

Let peace like a phoenix rise again . . .

On the rubble and the pain, send a healing rain
Let your love, let it smile again

Nobody seems to listen although they use your name.
Lord, your death seems all in vain,

Let peace like a phoenix rise again . . .

Garth Hewitt
England

Where There Is No Peace (2)

Then the General called for Law and Order,
  'Let the mob learn how to behave.'
And the President ordered,
  'Stop your disturbing reports in the press.'
And the Judges got together and said,
  'We will punish all disturbers of the peace.'
And the Corporation published its view,
  'Peace and Prosperity touch the Balance Sheet together.'

'Peace, peace, where there is no peace,'
is the cry of every oppressor.
Help us, God of Hope, not to pretend,
not to confuse self-interest,
but to seek that peace which rests
on respect for all your children everywhere.

Bernard Thorogood
Australia

War (1)

Around my feet there lie
Crude rough dug mounds of earth,
Dry cracking in the sun
And staked – as through the heart –
With splintered wood, red-number daubed,
Deep driven in the ground . . .

No sound is here,
And brazen sun seals sorrow in
To the farthest margined edges –
Dry and tearless.

My standing shadow
Intersects the upright of the stake,
And sharply shapes the symbol of a cross
Upon the silence . . .

Was there not another cross like this before
Long years ago?
Was there not other mocking and mourning
Disfiguring the fleeting of the years
With pock-marked venom?
Have we learned nothing
Through the ageing of the time –
That we must ever stand at the sun baked graves
And, sorrowing, do penance?

Have we learned nothing?

Margot Arthurton
England

War (2)

How does one man shout to a million
That blue eyes and light hair are best . . .
That the rest are nothing
And only good for ridding?
Why did the million believe,
And how?
And now
Have we learned so little
In our following time
That otherness is still a fear
To contemplate beyond the laws of reason?

153

How many seasons must we pass
Towards a future
Where diversity breeds only love,
And needs no learning to persuade it?
How many?

Many . . .

Margot Arthurton
England

Movements Against War

God of Peace,
we cannot be but profoundly shocked at savage terrorist
    attacks
and deeply concerned by the global culture of violence of
    which these attacks are a symptom.
We thank you for growing public condemnation of war,
with all the suffering it is causing in civilian deaths,
destruction of homes and the plight of refugees fleeing from
    bombing.
May politicians see beyond the simple aim of catching and
    punishing terrorists
and put their energies into discovering and removing the
    causes of hostility and alienation from which terrorism
    springs.

Alan Litherland
England

War Violates

In peace children bury their parents. War violates the order of
nature and causes parents to bury their children.

Herodotus

Humanity . . . Inhumanity

What is man,
Who in his inspiration,
Can paint the spark of God upon a chapel roof,
And leave a song of symphonies
Unto the earth?
Who, faced with Nature's mightiest creation,
Will scale the heights with courage to the end,
And still extend, in quiet humiliation,
A helping hand unto his weaker friend?

What is man, who, in retaliation,
Relinquishes nobility, and to the depths descends
Of infinite depravity
Without a thought?
Who, for the sake of colour, creed, or nation –
Fanatical unto his dying breath –
Leads prisoners out, and for extermination
Sets dogs on them to tear them all to death?

We may share with man his mighty aspiration . . .

But we must also bear his shame.

Margot Arthurton
England

Wasteland

What have we done to our land?
Shattered our homes,
Shattered our people,
Scattered their blood
And ravaged the land.

Ravaged and savaged our land –
Churned up our fields,
Laid waste our towns,
Blood-run our rivers –
And ruined our land.

What is this rage we have wrought?
Breaking our lives,
Breaking our hearts,
Fighting our friends –
Losing all, and for naught.

Agony screams from our land –
Blasted by bombs,
Murdered by mines,
Shattered by shells –
From our own hand.
What have we done to our land?

Margot Arthurton
England

The Playground Was a War Zone

The little child watched,
    and anger grew.
The playground was a war zone,
    with enemies, known and not-yet-known, everywhere.
The school day brought a series of skirmishes,
    with sabotage, hijack and ambush (real and imagined).
Words were amongst the most powerful weapons deployed,
    although fists and well-timed feet played their part.

The little child tried hiding,
    or playing sick,
        but the camouflage never lasted.

In time the little child found a way of coping.

156

The secret lay in hunting down another child even smaller,
  even weaker,
    even more afraid.

Neil Thorogood
England

Treasure

One fine morning, the child stood on the lawn
covered with daisies and dandelions,
and hardly dared breathe for beauty.
The grass was thick around her ankles and in it,
as far as she could see, were jewels laid out
on spring-green velvet.

Each daisy was a perfect yellow cushion
edged with white petals, some blush tinted.
Every dandelion was made from sunshine,
and some had on their faces, wet diamonds
that shivered and glittered when they rolled
onto the child's fingers.

She took a bunch of this perfect treasure
in to her father and he admired every flower,
his eyes growing soft with memory.
Together, they put them in a glass
on the kitchen windowsill which instantly
became a shrine to beauty.

Later that day, someone said, 'Nice lawn.
It's a pity there are so many weeds in it.
I have a spray that'll get rid of them.'
At that moment, the child learned
that when a treasure is judged a weed
it has no value at all.

Joy Cowley
Aotearoa New Zealand

Child of War

Child, child,
Wide eyed child –
Face aged in pain
The world's child –
Lost –
Innocence bearing sin,
Harbouring fear –
Alone
Unprotected
Orphan child . . .
Child of war.

Margot Arthurton
England

The Only Way?

War
    releases me
        from the burden
            of loving my neighbours
                and trying to understand them.

War
    allows me
        the freedom
            to ignore
                the bonds of humanity.

War
    teaches me
        the right of might
            the folly of love
                the weakness of dreams.

War
   asks me
      a question:
         Must this be
            the only way?

Neil Thorogood
England

We Had to Fight

We had to fight.
Lord, we could not see another way
to halt the tyrant
to release the prisoners
to stop the cruelty
to chain the madman.

But it was a terrible business,
a blood-red page of history,
written in pain and sorrow.
The innocent were caught,
screaming, in the net of war.

Lord, we fought because we did not know
   a better way,
and yet we sense in your design
   a saner day.
Wisdom, light, courage, hope
   for all we pray.

Bernard Thorogood
Australia

War Zone
Habakkuk 1:1–4, 2:1–4

God, it's a war zone
  people are beaten up
shot at, murdered in the streets
and you do nothing to stop it.

  People disappear
and are found in mass graves
  broken and mutilated,
    and there is no justice.

God of peace, this is a place of terror;
  God of love, this is a time of hate.

We pray today for war correspondents who stand at the
  flashpoints of the world and look for the truth.
Give them clear vision and help them to be faithful in
  recording what they see
so that those who hold your vision of justice and peace
may work and wait for it to be real
in every war zone which is also
GodZone
God's own.

Heather Pencavel
England

San Carlos Water

*'San Carlos Water' was written for a Remembrance Day Service in
1983, the year of the Falklands War. It was originally a song, for
which my son, Stuart, wrote the music, and he sang it for the first time
on that occasion. In a sense, therefore, it is limited to that event, but
perhaps it also echoes some of the futility of the conflicts in which the
young men and women of our nation have been embroiled since then.*

Set loose the iron wings of war at Freedom's proud command,
And obey the call to battle that you do not understand;
For who may read the future from the hollow of his hand
As time and tide run swiftly like sifted grains of sand –
While the winter wind is wailing and the salt snow stings with
	tears;
And the waves break white across San Carlos water.

Close the windows of your memory with the curtains of the
	rain,
For who is now to answer what was loss and what was gain?
Bleak on a barren hillside let scattered stones remain
To young men of the morning who will never wake again –
For the wild, white birds are crying as they bear against the
	gale,
And the storm-clouds roll across San Carlos water.

Come, raise the toast of victory to our great and glorious dead,
And on gilded scrolls of honour let their gallant names be
	read –
Though their laughter drift to silence in the ashes of your
	head,
In blood and water mingled, broken bodies, broken bread –
From the snowdrift and the burning, from the tidal waves of
	pain,
All their dreams lie lost beneath San Carlos water.

And the empty shells still echo with the voices of the sea,
From the mirage and the madness, who will dare to set us
	free?
Still the tempest tears the branches of a leafless, twisted tree –
Oh, when you come to Paradise, dear Lord, remember me.
For a lonely dove still hovers on the broken wings of peace,
In the dark of dawn across San Carlos water.

Jill Jenkins
England

161

Refugee

I am stood here –
Alone –
Surrounded by the sharpness
And the shattered edge of war . . .
For all around my young eyes to see
The easiness of old familiarity
Wrecked.

The sky intrudes upon the attic stair,
Exposing all,
And endless water drops incessantly –
Wasted;
Conscious of my thirst
I taste the dust amongst the taste of fear,
And, from somewhere, hear the hiss of gas.

There is a sort of deathly stillness here,
Surrounding me,
Distilled amongst the ruins of my place:
I wait for some small sound of other life
Within this broken space
That was my home . . .
But there is none.

And in the outside street
I see a flood of humanity –
Weeping and streaming
In its flight from fear
From here to where?
Their tears may lay the blood and dust of war,
But not allay the cost –
For all are lost, and flow directionless.

I join the flood and hope
That in its tired momentum

I may find again the small illusion
Of belonging.

Would there ever be another place
That I could know as home,
With constancy of water for my thirst,
And bread for my small hunger?
May I sleep some future night once more
In fearlessness?
And will there be warm arms
To hold me through the darkness of my dreams,
To understand my childish pain?
To let me rage again, again,
And quietly comprehend the awfulness
Of my life's dispossession?

If this shall be,
Then there is hope for me;
And finally
I'll understand, with childlike surety,
That in the sweetness of security
The purpose of my life shall be regained . . .

And with my childhood agonies contained –
I shall be healed.

Margot Arthurton
England

Lord, I Am in Pain

Lord, I am in pain.
Creator, we are aching.
Lord, we are overcome with horror.

I have watched and turned away
Numb, and speechless; frozen with impact,
Unwilling, unable to stand as silent witness.

We have tried to move, with impotent sympathy,
To pray, to light a candle, gesture in the dark.

And reality hits, O Lord,
Glimpses of individual horror, frantic choices,
Desperate hopes spill into our irrational minds.

Impotent anger moves to vengeance –
The choice is simple.

But, O Lord, you make me pause.

Creator who poured out creation
Creator who became created
Creator who accepted creation's sentence.

You make me pause and look at my blame.
You bring before me the even more unthinkable,

I, desperate, counter-creation to your Spirit
I, in greed, in silence and collusion,
Have been silent, inactive and unprotesting,
And I, too, have made the world a place for desperate evils.

Lord, have mercy.

Wendy White
England

In the Museum

In the museum was darkness
Where stark images
Stood in pools of black,
And voices telling
The terror of it all
And pain;
Again in every room

164

A spectre loomed
Of death and wickedness
And stunning horrors
Emanating from the mind of man –

And courage displayed
Quite without fuss . . .

All was to view –
Letters.
And small facets of the ordinary . . .
Nothing was spared.

Exposure was to capture us
Who shared the images
That shone from darkness,
The starkness of truth
Burning us the onlookers,
The learners –
Searing our souls like a brand
With scenes of no forgetting . . .
Letting our minds open a chink
And bringing to the brink
Of understanding
Our own selves . . .

Unforgettable.

Margot Arthurton
England

Where's the Glory, Hallelujah?

There's a stirring call to action as the tanks begin to roll,
and the battleships and fighter planes surge on towards their
  goal.

When the smart bombs find their targets there's a splendid
    show of force,
for the champion is riding out upon his shining horse.

Where's the glory, hallelujah?
Where's the glory, hallelujah?
Where's the glory, hallelujah?
When the champion goes riding out upon his shining horse.

But the legacy of battle lies in mines and cluster bombs,
where the limbless children play amid the wreckage of their
    homes
and the lifeless eyes of women hold the images they saw
when the blood-red horse rode over them, whose rider's name
    was War.

Where's the glory, hallelujah?
Where's the glory, hallelujah?
Where's the glory, hallelujah?
When the blood-red horse rides over them, whose rider's name is War.

In this bloated world of plenty, where the wheels of greed are
    oiled
so that millions are kept hungry on the lands that we have
    spoiled,
from the refugees in dust-filled camps we try to veil our sight –
for the rider's name is Famine and this horse is dark as night.

Where's the glory, hallelujah?
Where's the glory, hallelujah?
Where's the glory, hallelujah?
When the rider's name is Famine and the horse is dark as night.

When the deathly pale horse passes by, the world is gripped
    by fear,
seeing new diseases take a hold and old ones reappear,

when perverted use of knowledge gives new meaning to 'the
  beast'
and the toll of death and horror calls new vultures to the feast.

Where's the glory, hallelujah?
Where's the glory, hallelujah?
Where's the glory, hallelujah?
When the toll of death and horror calls the vultures to the feast.

But there is another vision of a city filled with light
where the desperate and persecuted have a home by right,
where resources for the healing of the nations can be found –
and the choice is ours! Our broken world could still be holy
  ground.

Where's the glory, hallelujah?
Where's the glory, hallelujah?
Where's the glory, hallelujah?
We can make the choice! Our broken world can still be holy ground.

Janet Wootton
England

The Two Faces of Peace

Stop the killings! Stop the bombs!
We pray that wars may end.
Yet human crime and national crime
continue through the ages.

God, may we end this bullying
in the human playground; may we grow up.
Teach us better ways of meeting hostility
and show us how to mediate
as Jesus showed the way and took the pain of it.

But peace of heart
   a settled mind,
   a single eye,
   a life made whole,
   a quietness in prayer,
   an assurance of tomorrow,
   a hand held firmly
   and an unassailable hope
is your grace in the Spirit.
Give us peace of heart today.

Bernard Thorogood
Australia

The Coming of Peace

Song of the Storm
(Luke 8:22–25)

I wake up in the sea,
I start to roar.
I fly up into the air,
sweeping across the sea.

A boat comes under me
I roar,
I start to make rain,
whirling the sea around as I power up.

I start to lash people with cold sea water,
screeching in their ears.
The sea is like a giant sea-monster
sweeping the boat about.

I thunder at them all.
But then the Son of God comes;

I feel all my power go . . .
Only a breeze remains of me.

Philip Fryar (aged ten)
England

He Is Dead . . .

Two women are sitting on stools/chairs, staring ahead, each holding a baby's jacket. They are each in their own world – remembering aloud.

Together He is dead . . . I have lost my son . . . he is dead.

Bethlehem mother Thirty-three years ago, it was.

Mary, mother of Jesus Three hours ago, it was.

Together My son is dead.

B.M. I have never forgotten the horror of it.

Mary I will never forget the horror of it.

B.M. We were overjoyed when I conceived.
We hoped upon hope our first-born would be a son.
How we cuddled and hugged each other!

Mary It was a difficult time when I became pregnant.
My fiancé, Joseph, wanted me to hide until the birth because of the shame.
But his mood soon changed and he shared my awe-struck delight at what had happened to me.

169

Together How we marvelled at the baby moving within
me!
How we dreamed and planned.
My son (if it was a son) would be a carpenter, just
like his dad.
My husband, Joseph, would make him his own
little set of tools
so that from an early age he could work by his
side.
We could just imagine it! Our little lad proudly
helping his dad.

B.M. He was born at home in Bethlehem.
A small house with a workshop on the side.
My friends came round when my birthpains
started, to support me as the birth progressed.
It was a busy time. The town was full of folk
coming in for the census.
I remember hearing Joseph talking outside with
the passers-by whilst our baby was born.
I remember, through the pain, hearing him
directing folk to the nearby inn.

Mary He was born in Bethlehem.
We'd had to travel back there – Joseph and me –
because of the census.
Bethlehem was his place of birth.
But we couldn't find anywhere to stay and my
birthpains had started.
Then we were directed to the inn and there we
were offered space in the stable with the
animals.
The only space they had left.
And there I gave birth.
It was a lonely experience with no friends or
family to support me through the ordeal. Only
good, faithful Joseph – and the animals!

B.M. There was great rejoicing.
All our friends came to visit and brought presents
for our special baby.
This jacket was one of them.
As news spread more and more folk dropped in.
How the small town echoed to the sounds of
rejoicing.

Mary How the small town echoed to the sounds of
rejoicing.
Angels sang.
Shepherds and kings visited and brought gifts.
The innkeeper's wife came in with this little jacket
which had belonged to her son.
And the news spread and soon others were
popping their heads round the stable door to
see our special baby.

Together It was a boy.

B.M. We named him James.

Mary We named him Jesus.

Together How we treasured those first weeks.
Watching God's good gift to us – our little
James/Jesus – how time-consuming it was.
First just feeding and changing him.
And marvelling over him.
Then his personality began to appear.
And his first smile.
How that first smile is engraved on my heart.

B.M. And then . . . well, and then the soldiers came!
I have lain awake night after night going over and
over the events of that night and day of horror.
No words can describe it.

How could God do this to us?
Our son murdered.
Battered to death, his head split open, by order of
    the king.
And he was not the only one.
His only crime?
Being the first-born son – and being under two
    years old.
Where is the justice in that?
My brain echoes with the screams of the babies.
My heart breaks as it hears again the sound of
    wailing.
And then the silence.
The deadly, eerie silence.
No mother should see her son die.
Where was God in all this?
Where was he?
Was this really necessary to fulfil some old
    prophecy?
My heart was breaking . . . breaking . . .

Mary   And then . . . well, then we had to flee.
To Egypt.
Then word reached us that all the first-born sons
    under two years old in Bethlehem had been
    killed as Herod had sent the soldiers in search
    of our son.
Were we really the cause of all that murder?
All that heartbreak?
I couldn't bear it!
It seemed difficult to work out God's plan for us
    when we heard this.
Later we returned home.
Jesus grew into a fine young man.
    All along he had loved helping Joseph in his
    workshop.
Using his hands. Making things.

I remember the first little box he made . . . he was
   so proud.
I have it still.
His father died . . . and when his brothers and
   sisters were grown, he left home.
'To do his heavenly Father's business.'
He was baptized by his cousin. He went into the
   desert.
And at the end of forty days, he returned –
   knowing what his mission was to be and to
   whom he was sent.
The outcast, the unlovely, the unloved.
To bring down the powerful and the proud.
I would hear of his travels, of his teaching and his
   healing.
Of his loyal band of disciples.
Of how the crowds followed him, day after day.
And from time to time I would see him.
But only rarely . . .

B.M.   We had no more children.
My husband died too soon.
He died of a broken heart.
All our dreams lost in one brutal act.
It's only in the last few months – that I have
   seemed to come alive again.
I've been following that great teacher, Jesus.
I have heard him teach.
He makes such sense.
What's more – I've seen how he loves.
Oh, how he loves!
I was even able, in one rare, quiet moment, to
   share with him my despair, my bitterness, my
   anger.
And he took me in his arms.
And he hugged me better.
He took from me the bitterness which over the

173

years had gnawed away at me turning my heart
into stone.

And my heart melted – and became ready to
respond to the need in others.

Mary And in the end he made so many enemies that it
has come to this.

My son is dead.

That entry into Jerusalem and the cheering
crowds meant nothing.

It was pointless.

For how could folk welcome him one minute –

And be prepared to shout 'Crucify him' the next?

How could they?

Where was God in all this?

Where was he.

I sat at the foot of the cross, weeping.

And, even in his agony, Jesus tried to comfort me.

But no mother should see her son die.

Certainly not on a cross.

They shouldn't have nailed my son to a cross.

Was this really necessary to fulfil some old
prophecy?

My heart is breaking . . . breaking . . .

B.M. And I followed him into Jerusalem.

What an entry that was.

I shouted 'Hosanna' and waved a palm leaf with
the best of them.

But it came to nothing.

Meant nothing.

For how could folk welcome him one minute –

And be prepared to shout 'Crucify him' the next?

How could they?

Where was God in all this?

Where was he.

I followed the crowd to where they crucified him.

174

Crucified the one who had saved me.
My saviour.
And I saw a woman there.
I'm sure it was his mother.
No mother should see her son die.
Certainly not nailed to a cross.
They shouldn't have nailed her son to a cross.
My heart is bleeding for her.
What can I say to her?
How can I comfort her?
 (Moves to put arms round Mary)

Together   My son is dead.

Liz Davies
England

Forgive Our Foolish Ways

It is written, O Lord,
That the prayer of the righteous has much power,
That the Word of truth has great authority.

Who, O Lord, is righteous in Your eyes?
Who can stand before You equal in holiness?
The one whose tongue forms no evil,
Whose hand works no wickedness.

Look upon the folly of Your creation, O Lord,
See with Your own eyes
The high moral purpose
We have claimed for ourselves.

We are at war again
Nation upon nation
Raging and foaming at the mouth,
Destruction reigns in the desert.

175

We are slaves to the pride that possesses us,
Servants of the greed that drives us.
Everyone wants to live by his own law.
Each one listens only to his own voice.

We speak high-sounding words to cover our low motives.
We define great deeds to hide low esteem.
We seek our own fame,
Daring to believe that such a thing
Will outlast Your glory.
We have turned our backs to Your face.
And scorned Your great salvation.

I cannot presume to speak Your great word, O Lord.
I come before You knowing my complicity in the common
    folly of humanity.
Though my prayer be imperfect,
I appeal to Your grace.
Let me claim a portion of Your mercy,
And rejoice that You perfect my petitions.
If it were not for Your mercy, O Lord,
Who could stand before You at all?

Forgive our foolish ways.
Break the pride that fuels ambition.
Crush the greed that rules our actions.

Robert Anderson
England

Jesus, We Need to Talk

Jesus, we need to talk!
It's about the news.
There's just so much of it that's bad.
I never seem to get through a day without yet another act of
    violence being pushed at me.

If it isn't some ghastly war grinding on in some barely-heard-
of corner of the world it's a high-profile killing on a slick
city street.
Or it's some new invention that offers the chance for even
greater slaughter and a good profit forecast for investors.
Then there's the regular, sordid, flood of domestics with
families laying into each other and doing unimaginable
things.
And what about the refugees who huddle on my screen and
stare at me with eyes that hold too many tragedies for me to
handle?
It's getting me down.
It makes me despair.
So what are you doing about it, Jesus?
An answer would be good.
Just a word or two, a sign, a bit of hope.

Is that it?

'Follow me.'

Neil Thorogood
England

Seasons of Forsakenness

Why forsake us, O Forsaking One –
We who surrender all to follow You?
What motivates You to seem elusive,
To withdraw from us
O Bewildering One,
From us who feel we cannot survive or thrive
Without a conscious presence of Very You?

Where is our harvest of joy,
Of seeds sown in tears
Sown and tilled over long years
When you seem not anywhere, seem not to care?
'Forsake all for me' You said.

We do. We did. And so do You seem to
Forsake us
In the dark years of severe mercy,
Dark decades of corruption and injustice;
Dark eras of unremitting poverty;
During the dark centuries of dust-in-the-mouth,
Dust-in-the-eyes, dust-in-the-soul experiences
Causing a dry rot, spirit-sapping toll
For any and all so involved.
Darkest mystery of
Dark Mystery.

You, the Forsaken Christ of the Dark Cross
Who sank deepest deep
Encountering those who had sunk into evil's blackness
Into eternal lostness.
You, the Forsaken Christ, transformed the void by being
deepest dark
So utterly dark to the uttermost
That Christ Forsaken-by-the-Father-Dark out-darked
Dark Evil.
Thus was evil enlightened?
Thus was evil redeemed
Through Light-of-God-not-there
Through Dark-of-God-yet there?

Oho! Are we discerning that
Christ-Forsakenness out-darks our darkness
To bring in a harvest of re-forming souls?
And, in the refining process, asks that we, in turn,
Know forsakenness
As being necessary to the beloving of our dark-light nature,
To the be-loving of all others?

Perhaps. If so,
Pierce our black anguish, Beloving One,
By planting tough seed in us,
The gutsy seed of hope,

The swelling seed of trust
Which grow best
In apparent abandonment
In our seasons of forsakenness.

Glenn Jetta Barclay
Aotearoa New Zealand

Now Is the Time

Sharing the life of the living,
sharing our faith and our doubts,
sharing the gifts God is giving,
sharing the new hope that sprouts,
sharing the longing for justice,
sharing the vision for peace,
sharing in witness and service
sharing abundance and needs:

Now, now is the time:
be reconciled, people to people.
Now, now is the time:
live a new life in balance with earth.
We are in Christ all reconciled;
churches with churches, each one to God.

Sharing our long, winding story,
sharing like pilgrims our food,
sharing the songs of God´s glory,
sharing the trust in the good,
sharing our birth and our ageing,
sharing the joy and the pain,
sharing the mirth and the raging,
sharing the grace of the grain:

Now, now is the time. . . .

Per Harling
Sweden

Loss

*Dedicated to a woman weeping in a church after returning from the
inquest of her son whose body had been found on a railway line*

I cannot bear to think that you would choose
To lie on cruel steel to die,
My precious one . . .
That you would steal away
Some lonely day
And, silent, let your fretful spirit loose.

There is a child in all of us
That needs to weep,
That feels the pain of life,
The grief and strife of head and heart
That tears the soul apart.

I share that element of child with you
My fledgling son –
For in your going you did borrow
All my joy to ease your way –
And leave me only sorrow.

What agony was yours unshed, unshared,
Which of your very essence did destroy?
What weariness of life?
What legacy of questions unresolved?

Only your space remains –
An absent presence shadowing the sun,
The moon, the stars, the ancient Earth –
Your present absence echoes wordless pains,
But gives no clues
Why you would choose
To lie upon cruel steel to die.

Margot Arthurton
England

180

Spring in Hell

Blue sky high
White clouds racing,
Chasing the wind
Air crystal clear,
Sun warm and beckoning.
I am swept into
The mood of spring
And feel I want
To shout and sing.

But no words come.
For I can see the faces
Of those compelled to flee
From home and warmth and comfort
Into void.

Young women carrying infants,
Small children clinging on,
Exhausted and distraught,
Fearing the worst has happened
To their men.

Old folk now frail and fragile
Blindly struggling to stumble on
With nothing left to grasp
Not even a hope.

Scared mothers giving birth
On a cold damp muddy field.
Is this modern Bethlehem
Two thousand years ahead?

Can I ever again feel the urge
To dance and sing for joy
And watch my brothers, sisters
Crushed to death?

Kathleen Davey
Northern Ireland

Sold Short

You came breathing peace
offering hands full of love, saying
'Come into the light, leave darkness behind
follow me as we dance in the morning dew.'
They came spewing hatred,
crazed minds, blind eyes, cruel hands,
to kiss you with death.
Crucify, crucify, they insist.
Not knowing in killing you
they welcome their own death.
Choosing darkness, crushing life,
rushing into an abyss of bitterness.
Sold for thirty pieces of silver.
Sold short, but who?

Wendy D. Ward
Aotearoa New Zealand

Yearning for God

This is London
Where the signs all read
Labourers – no vacancies;
Job Centre – no vacancies;
Hostels – no vacancies;
Bed and breakfast – no vacancies.

People's hearts also have no vacancies
For many here are full –
Full of sadness, anger, anxiety and weariness.
In the snack bar I see eyes
Staring blankly over lengthy cups of tea.
This is the city
Like Bethlehem – once
Yearning for help and direction and love:

Yearning for God to come in the flesh,
And make a difference.
Not a historical story of long ago.
Not statistics to be announced in the news,
But real people loved by you,
With crushed lives.

I have a feeling, Lord,
You've been here before.

Martin Wallace
England

Longing for Silence

You tell me that this City of Earth
Is to reflect your City of Heaven.
But reality is my neighbours:
When the parents work on night shift
Their children hold a noisy party
Until 6 am Sunday morning.
The police call three times
And then give up.
Other neighbours
Shut their dog in the yard
All night
Barking loudly!
But not as loudly
As the couple who argue
At the top of their voices
All night long.
And then Lord
There is the crazy woman
Who walks the street in her nightie
Shouting at the world
While her neighbours
From their bedroom window

Pour on her their scorn
And the contents of their baby's potty.
And your Word tells me in Revelation,
'There was silence in Heaven for half an hour.'
Lord –
Take me now!

Martin Wallace
England

Neighbours

Two seriously affluent semis
eye each other.

Pseudo gas lamp-post
versus
three white pawnbroker globes:
one all.

Decorative brick paving.
Decorative brick paving.
White plastic flower tubs.
White plastic flower tubs.
No change.

Red quasi Victorian postbox:
two-one!

Entire house-front jungled
with flowering climbers:
regains lead.

Jungle transformed:
a thousand white
glow-worm lights, some flashing in synchrony,
some twinkling randomly,

a thousand more inside
on Xmas trees and furniture,
leaving hardly any room
for people.
Well ahead now.

But on the other side
in the twilight,
projecting from roof corner
a branch,
menacing,
ready to launch a bulb-salvo.
And
its owner
lurks at bay
in the bay,
poised
to strike
and WIN.

Geoffrey Herbert
England

Jericho Road

I was so neat and tidy as I bustled into the station,
And the sun was high in the sky,
Hotly drenching that city of London,
And I so neat and tidy, with a train to catch
And a job to be done,
I and a million others.

It was in the entrance I saw him,
Not unusually in any big city,
Curled in a heap of helplessness,
In the sleep of a man defeated

185

A body distorted, a body abused,
And I , so neat and tidy,
As I bustled into the station,
With a train to catch and a job to be done.
I stopped and stared at this hideous human,
Oh God! A brother of mine!
And he didn't see me as I stumbled away,
Draped in a cloak of shame
And I was so neat and tidy with a train to catch
And a job to be done –
Oh God, a brother of mine!

Pamela Klimcke
Ireland

In Situations of Abuse

God, I feel so alone, so cut off, so shut out.
I can't relate to you as 'Lord', 'Almighty Father', 'Eternal
    King'.
I can't cope with your power and authority, as I have none.
I am frightened of your otherness.

But as Jesus, loving friend who valued those who were shut
    out,
who was condemned and tortured himself, I can approach you.
As Holy Spirit who cuddles us to her breast,
who inspires us with courage, I can approach you.

Please hold me tight; heal my broken body and battered spirit.
Empower me with the knowledge of your love and belief
so that I may learn to value that I am made in your image
and worth so much more than I dare contemplate.

I pray for the strength to love myself enough to leave the
    abuse.

I ask that you bring the reality of the resurrection into my life,
that your fire and joy will blossom into a new life of love,
   justice, hope and peace.
Amen.

Zam Walker
Wales/Scotland

Unconditional Love

One time a beggar woman with cancer of the face tried to kiss
Dorothy Day's hand. Dorothy commented: 'The only thing I
could do was kiss her dirty old face with the gaping hole in it
where an eye and nose had been. It sounds like a heroic deed
but it was not. What we avert our eyes from today can be borne
tomorrow when we have learned a little more about love.'

'Without unconditional love there can be no peace in the heart,
and without peace in the heart, there can be no peace in the
world.'

Source Unknown

All-knowing God

All-knowing God, we follow your instructions to lay our problems at your feet. We pray for those wrestling with issues of
war and peace. These matters are never clear-cut and violent
reactions are not the way to bring peace, yet evil must be
defeated – and there is so much evil in the world. We pray for
all people of influence and power. Open their minds to con-
structive ways of peacemaking and resolving conflict.

Marjorie Dobson
England

Father, Forgive Them

Bless those innocent victims of war, who have no place to go to escape it and no homes to go to when it all ends. Bless those whose job it is to fight when they are told – and especially bless those who fight for a cause they don't understand, urged on by people with evil motives. Father, forgive them, for they don't know what they are doing.

Marjorie Dobson
England

Bless Those Who Mourn

We pray for people who are battling with grief and especially those who feel that the death of their loved one was unjust. For them there is anger, as well as sorrow; regret, bewilderment, fear and an aching hole filled only with tears. Jesus, you wept at the death of a friend and we weep too. But in the battle to cope they have you as an ally. Soldiers who were only following orders killed your son Jesus unjustly. You understand this grief as one who went through it. Bless those who mourn, Lord, and comfort them. For your Son's sake.
Amen.

Marjorie Dobson
England

Endings

'This is the end,'
Said Moses
As he saw the Red Sea cross his path,
A barrier to freedom.
And yet today
The Jews still celebrate their crossing
As a turning point
Within their history.

'This is the end,'
Said Elijah
Hiding in his mountain cave,
Cowering from danger.
And yet, from there,
Through howling wind and storming rain
He saw God's power
Within the stillness.

'This is the end,'
Said Mary
Bent with sorrow at the cross's foot
Where hung her son.
And yet she heard
'Take care of her,' and felt his love
Surround her even then
Within the arms of John.

'This is the end,'
Said Jesus
As his tortured body gave itself to death
And darkness fell.
And yet he knew
This end was but a new beginning.
No power of Rome or Jew could keep the love of God
Within a tomb.

'This is the end,'
We say
When life is torn apart
By tragic loss.
And yet, beyond our grief,
The pain-filled eyes of a Father,
Whose Son faced death too soon,
Are weeping with us.

Marjorie Dobson
England

Christ Among the Crucified

Do you think that was the *first* time he saw Golgotha
the day they nailed him up?
Surely the Son of Man was sometime to be found
in the place of the skull
among sinners and the felons and the dead
speaking, past pain, of the *now* of the Kingdom of God.

I think of Christ touching even these unclean,
healer, teacher, lover of broken souls,
talking with guards in their evil duty,
promising forgiveness to the criminal,
as legs were broken and they choked and died.
Did he think, 'There but for the grace of God, go I?'

Did he see then in their suffering his own pathway,
the bloody night in Gethsemane? Did he know
precisely what he asked of God (and was denied)?
How more extraordinary then, his walk to agony,
the promise to the thief of paradise,
his acceptance of the nails and the spear.

If he had been before and seen that end
among the blood and flies and degradation
so sanitized by us, if he knew *exactly*
how long each could hang in the sun,
what possessed him then to take the donkey
and ride so publicly into Jerusalem?

I think it was the love of humankind
overwhelmed him, there among the crucified.
Their drowning, suffering, gasping, bleeding out,
all the ways we humans have to die,
required him to do more than pass among them
and so become them, taking on their fate.

And if God raised this Jesus from all that sweat,
the stink of fear, the terror of our end,
then we can believe in hope of lasting peace,
beyond struggle and injustice and lives gone wrong.
It is what keeps us going, beyond eternal life,
when today we walk among the crucified.

Anne Richards
England

Peace Prayer

When
The rhythm of life
Is death
And each breath
A smoke-filled tear;
When the siren sings
The songs of lullaby:

Grant us your peace.

When
Humanness
Is trampled
And lives are
The currency we spend;
When the stench of death
Rises with the morning sun: .

Grant us your peace.

When
The darkness
Is unending
And each wall seems
Unyielding;

When hope and despair conflict
In ever-deepening fray:

Grant us your peace

That we may anchor our souls
In the One who is just,
Who renews our strength
For the work to be done;
May we look up
To the One who is peace:

O Lord,
Grant us your peace.

Claire Smith
Guyana

Chapter Five
Working for Peace

God Blesses Those Who Work for Peace

'God blesses those who work for peace,
    for they are called the children of God.'

Thank you for the invitation and the promise, Father.
Thank you for taking this appalling risk,
    entrusting into our fickle hands the seeds of peace,
        encouraging us to scatter them widely and wisely and
            well.
Thank you for the promise of your blessing,
    for assuring us of our worth in your eyes and our place at
        your side,
        for naming us your children,
            cherished, protected and known.

You call us to work for you.
So put us to work.
Put us to work where hope evaporates in the blinding heat of
        hate.
Put us to work when lives are crippled by wars fought or wars
        rehearsed.
Put us to work as peace slips through the fingers of our
        leaders.
Put us to work if peace is drowning beneath evil words and
        sinister ideas.

Put us to work, Father.
And, when the work is hard and long,
    remind us of your blessing and renew our hope.
In the name of Jesus Christ we ask it.
Amen.

Neil Thorogood
England

195

The Things that Make for Peace

There is a moment when we see that peace is real.

It can come in our homes,
   it can be a guest at our conference tables and in our board
      rooms,
   it can slip across a frontier drawn on the land or carved into
      a human heart,
   it can blossom in a devastated community.

There can be a sudden awakening to the truth of someone
      else's hurt,
   there can be a new-found art of listening,
   there can be a confession that heals,
   there can be a vision that entrances everyone.

So it can be, living God.
So it is that in many ways your Spirit moves and works,
   and peace dawns.
May your Spirit move and work in us!
May we know the things that make for peace,
   and offer you our lives in service to your will.
In the name of Jesus Christ our Lord,
   who did the same.
Amen.

Neil Thorogood
England

Stand Up for Truth and Justice

Holy God,
Holy and One,
We bless you
   for creating all people
   different and in your image –
   black and white,
   female and male,

with all our different
colours, shapes and sizes,
gifts, languages and abilities.

We bless you
for the ways in which
you reach people
throughout the world.

We bless you
for all the ways in which
people respond to you
throughout the world.

Forgive us all
for the part we play
in mocking your holiness,
dividing your unity,
denying your presence
beyond our own experience,
and for launching an assault
on your image in others
and ourselves.

We hold before you
all those who suffer
because of religious and racial bigotry
and hatred.
Cast out of our being
and the world
the demons and terror of racism.
Send your prophets to speak out
and to stand up for truth and justice.
In the name of Christ.
Amen.

Inderjit S. Bhogal
Kenya/England

Stand and Be Counted

Creator God, father and mother of us all, we ask your forgiveness for our blindness, for not understanding that violence breeds violence, and for not doing anything about it when we do understand. Help us to lose our fear of testifying to the way of peace by giving our fear over to you so that we may 'stand and be counted'. We know in our hearts that true peace is rooted in prayer and is received into our innermost being by your grace and your grace alone. Help us to seek the Christ-like self within us and to rid ourselves of self-importance and selfishness, so that we may be as empty vessels into which you may pour your healing grace so as to bring peace into our hearts, our families, our communities, our nations, our world. Amen.

Nia Rhosier
Wales

Astoundingly Patient God

Astoundingly patient God
remain with us:

> so that we may live in hope
> that the church
> – the people of God –
> will put sympathetic awareness into loving action;

> so that we may live in hope
> that the people of God
> will put off their masks of respectability
> and take on the face of suffering humankind;

> so that we may live in hope
> that the people of God
> will see Christ in the faces
> of women and men who are victims of war;

198

so that we may live in hope
that the people of God
will denounce weapons of war
and speak out against the hypocrisy of
   the arms trade;

so that we may live in hope
that worshipping communities
will be motivated by urgent compassion,
   to rise up
      to go out
         to be courageous
            to put off the plaster casts of
            'we must not become involved'
            and
            to get their hands dirty and serve people,

as we make serious attempts
to bring in
some of the ways for Peace;
and get somewhere near the Kingdom of God – here on earth.

Geoffrey Duncan
England

Prayer to Our Blessed Virgin

Mary, Mother of Jesus and of those who participate in his
   priestly ministry, we come to you with the same attitude of
   children who come to their mother.
We are no longer children, but adults who desire with all our
   hearts to be God's children.
Our human condition is weak, that is why we come to ask for
   your motherly aid so we are able to overcome our
   weakness.

Pray for us so that we can, in turn, become people of prayer.
We invoke your protection so that we may remain free from
all sin.
We invoke your love so that it may reign and we will be able
to be compassionate and forgiving.
We ask for your blessing so we can be like the image of your
beloved Son, our Lord and Saviour, Jesus Christ. Amen.

Mother Teresa
India

Prayer of Rabindranath Tagore

This is my prayer to you, O Lord – strike at the root of penury
in my heart.
Give me the strength lightly to bear my joys and sorrows.
Give me the strength to make my love fruitful in service.
Give me the strength never to disown the poor or bend my
knees before insolent might.
Give me the strength to raise my mind high above daily trifles.
And give me the strength to surrender my strength to your
will with love.

Rabindranath Tagore
India

Build Peace

Build peace in the shanty towns
where children play in the rutted paths
and water is an hour distant.
Build peace on the hacienda
where a week's hard labour is rewarded
with a wage that cannot keep the family for a day.

200

Build peace in the divided village
where neighbour eyes neighbour with distrust and fear
born of last year's massacre.
Build peace in the land with people of three faiths
but with no agreement to share resources fairly
or to give hope for tomorrow amidst the crises of today.
Build peace where the reality is found in bombs and bullets;
where hate divides and despair fills hearts.
To build peace in such barren places
we will need the bricks of love and rocks of faith.

John Johansen-Berg
England

Love Is the Only Way
After the Basis of the Fellowship of Reconciliation

We celebrate the way
by which we know today
God's way is clear:
power for right's victory,
base of community,
hope for eternity –
sovereign Love here!

Here we accept the call
accepting each and all
as loved-ones too;
taking the risks involved
to get earth's problems solved
by means God has resolved
for us to do.

Love is the only way
to live at peace today
and ever more.

201

Faithful to Christ's command,
true to our native land,
for all the world we stand
resisting war.

Spirit of power and grace,
transcending time and space,
Christ now . . . Christ here;
waiting for us to see
that Christian love can be
saving society
from want and fear.

Express God's better way
through human lives today
to heal dis-ease;
conform us to God's will,
reform our natures still,
inform our thinking till
all live in peace.

David J. Harding
England

To Enter into Your Divinity

To refuse to struggle against the evil of the world
is to surrender your humanity;
to struggle against the evil of the world
with the weapons of the evildoer
is to enter into your humanity;
to struggle against the evil of the world
with the weapons of God
is to enter into your divinity.

Mahatma Gandhi
India

202

Someday . . .

Someday the demand for disarmament by hundreds of millions will, I hope, become so universal and so insistent that no man, no nations, can withstand it.

President Dwight D. Eisenhower
USA

Theft

Every gun that is made, every warship that is launched, every rocket that is fired signifies a theft from those that hunger and are not fed, from those who are cold and are not clothed.

President Dwight D. Eisenhower
USA

Candles

'Better to light a candle
than to curse the darkness'

But where are those lighted candles?
We grope around, not knowing
Which way to go –
Just darkness and half darkness.
We follow one glimmer of light
And reaching it
It flickers out.

More knee-cappings, blast bombs,
Mortar attacks, burnings,
Intimidation, protests
Just as before.
Are we too close to see in right perspective,
Too myopic to see beyond the 'now'?

Could we but wing our way
Across the heavens
And look at earth
Millions of miles away
Would we not see
A blaze of lighted candles
Girdling our planet
North, south, east and west?

Let us take heart,
All is not gloom,
For the darkest of nights
Precedes a new dawn.

Kathleen Davey
Northern Ireland

A Candle

This candle is red
like the blood of the victim,
a symbol of persecution.
Light it in faith
praying for justice.

This candle is green
like the grass in the fields,
a symbol of creation.
Light it in faith,
praying for renewal.

This candle is white,
like the snow on the hills,
a symbol of holiness.
Light it in faith,
praying for peace.

John Johansen-Berg
England

Quilt of Peace

Today, O Living God,
I offer a quilt of peace
Made from various colours, shapes and designs
Sewn together by rainbow people
In common aspiration
For Earth's survival.

Bless the peace process
Bless the peace-quilters
Bless the peace-makers
Bless the peace-dreamers
Bless, bless, bless. Amen.

Elizabeth Tapia
The Philippians

Lord of Life and Peace

Lord of Life and Peace
help us to be more aware,
now –
today
of the many faces of Peace waiting to be pursued.
In the present turmoil, with our diverse cultures
(name places in the current world news),
you know that we become overwhelmed,
and we get our priorities quite wrong.
Keep us well-balanced as we take positive action for Peace
and support suffering women, men and children wherever
    they are.

Enable us to be more informed; increase our understanding;
lead us to greater wisdom and compassion. Prompt and prod
us to be spiritually more open for gospel-action and to see the

face of Christ in the stranger. Lord of Life, Love and Peace, hear our prayers and act upon them as you will.
Amen.

Geoffrey Duncan
England

Fill Me with the Spirit of Peace

Blessed Lord Jesus Christ, may your prayers be my example when I pray through you to the Father. Early and late, fill me with the spirit of peace, so that I may find calm in the storms of the world and quiet in the noise of every day, to be renewed for the service to which you have called me.

Raymond Chapman
England

Help Us, O Christ, to Live the Way
A paraphrase of the prayer of St Francis

Help us, O Christ, to live the way of peace,
To bind the broken with compassion's bands,
To sow the seeds of love instead of hate,
To free the prisoner from oppressing hands.

Where doubt abides, O God, may we share faith,
Replace despair with hope's empowering song.
Where darkness dwells, may we bring healing light,
When grief descends help broken hearts feel strong.

O Christ, may we all seek to understand
Much more than to be fully understood;
Consoling all before we seek their care,
That they may know that life is truly good.

For through our giving we shall all receive,
Through our forgiving we shall find life's balm.
And in our letting go we all shall rise
To live the way of love and joyful calm.

Tune: Chilton Foliat

W. L. Wallace
Aotearoa New Zealand

Together in Peace

Creator God,
Lift the shadows of fear, of prejudice, of misunderstanding,
    from each of us,
And let us weave together in our country of Ireland,
A new Tapestry for living with our neighbour . . .
A Tapestry of new-born hope,
Woven with delicate threads of love.
May we be made as small children again,
Allowing ourselves to be made vulnerable in Your love,
And aware of our weakness.
And in drawing the warp and weft together,
Create a Tapestry of peoples that is tough and durable;
The Holy Spirit becoming the warp,
Strong in texture, supporting and strengthening,
Yet not so taut that the threads will break,
But pliable, giving, responsive to each other.
Release us from self, that together in peace,
We can come to You, united in Your love.
Amen.

Pamela Klimcke
Ireland

Bless the Peace-makers

God,
Bless the peace-makers.
Bless those who work in home and community to end a
     quarrel,
  bless those who keep faith with arguing churches,
  bless those who speak a careful word in corridors of power,
  bless those who live good and hopeful lives in refugee
     camps,
  bless those who minister to the military,
  bless those who seek peace with you and give your peace
     away.
Bless all our peace-makers with the powerful presence
  and support of your Holy Spirit,
  and the confidence that comes through following in the
     steps of Christ.
Amen.

Neil Thorogood
England

It Is Not Enough to Pray for Peace

It is not enough to pray for peace. We have to work for it: to
challenge those who foster conflict and refute their propaganda; to ascertain and make known the truth, both when it
confirms and when it runs counter to conventional views; to
denounce injustice, not only when it is committed against us
but also when it is committed against others; to defend human
rights, not only our own but also theirs; to insist that peace
requires sacrifice – of pride, or wealth, or territory; to practise
and promote the way of moderation, compromise and reconciliation; and to build bridges of respect and understanding,
trust and friendship, across the chasms that divide humanity.

Rabbi John D. Rayner
England

Lord, Speak ...

Lord, speak
   through the living word:

'Swords into ploughshares,
spears into pruning hooks.'

Yes,
but

landmines and cluster bombs
Kalishnikovs and AK 47s
keep the peace.

So we are told ...

by the dealers who make huge profits
from the death and destruction industry.

Lord, speak
   through the loving word:

'He has sent me to proclaim liberty to the captives
... to set free the oppressed.'

So, make us politely persistent in our pleading

to turn
weapons of war
into bore wells,
water pumps,
and irrigation systems.

Happy are the peace-makers
for they shall enable women and men
to experience justice

to know peace
and gain the benefits of healthy living.
Amen.

Geoffrey Duncan
England

In Your Name

Creator God, Father and Mother of all people,
May we speak freely and boldly . . . in Your name
May we allow ourselves to become vulnerable . . . in Your
    name
May we share our pain and our hopes . . . in Your name
May we honour each other . . . in Your name
May we know our strength and find our voice . . . in Your
    name
May we bless and be blessed . . . in Your name
And may we know that through all and in all,
Around, about, above and below,
God is with us.
Amen.

Pamela Klimcke
Ireland

God of Our Every Day

O God of our every day,
hold us in your sight, that we might learn to see,
in your presence, that we might learn to love,
in your peace, that we might learn to pray
for others, ourselves and all the world.

Julie M. Hulme
England

One World

Creator God, whose world is one family, help us to recognize our common humanity.

For wherever they are, victims of terrorism cry out in bitter anguish; bombs and shells kill soldiers and civilians alike; homes and businesses are shattered and broken; rescuers search rubble for faint signs of life; bereaved children weep bewildered tears; family units are torn apart by destruction; refugees lose their dignity and sense of identity; peace is shattered.

Keep us alert to the tears and fears that are our common experience. Open hands and hearts in sympathy and understanding. Show us how to express our care in practical ways. Please, Lord.

God of peace, whose world is torn apart by evil, greed, power and cruelty, help us to be active in our work for peace.

For all over your world power corrupts and greed distorts values; evil has no conscience; terrorists justify actions by perverted logic; prejudice feeds fear and fear promotes violence; weapons of mass destruction are dangerously active; ignorance promotes hostility, danger is at hand.

Help us to find the truth behind the propaganda. Teach us to promote peaceful ways and positive thoughts. Give us the courage to tackle prejudice where we find it. Show us how to face up to evil and defeat it. In your name, Lord and for your sake.

Marjorie Dobson
England

Shalom for Your People

Loving God,
when we offer asylum to the persecuted,
when we provide a home for the homeless,
when we feed the hungry
or provide wells for thirsty villagers,
there we offer your sign of peace,
shalom for your people.

John Johansen-Berg
England

Righteous Redeemer

Righteous Redeemer,
You have not counted the cost too great
in offering us a place in the kingdom of heaven.
May we seek to be alongside the poor and needy;
May we have a concern to offer food to the hungry;
May we not be tempted to pass by the oppressed;
May we not forget those who suffer from injustice.
Help us to play our part in building the kingdom of peace,
calling for a fair sharing of the earth's resources,
pleading the cause of the underprivileged,
rejecting the philosophy of hate and practice of
    discrimination.
So may we share together the good gifts of life
and find mutual encouragement in our common welfare
to the glory of your name
and for the establishing of true peace.

John Johansen-Berg
England

Responding to Our Neighbour's Need

I sought you, Lord, by still waters;
I searched for you in green fields;
I waited for you on the mountain's summit.
But I met you in the city's clamour;
I heard you in the orphan's cry;
I found you in the war-torn buildings.
Responding to our neighbour's need
we find your peace,
the peace that crosses barriers and unites nations.

John Johansen-Berg
England

Our Broken and Divided World

God of the nations, whose kingdom rules over all, have mercy on our broken and divided world. Shed abroad your peace in the hearts of men and women and banish from them the spirit that makes for war. Make the sufferings of our enemies intolerable to us and send us your Spirit for the binding up of each other's wounds. May our pain be joined with theirs so that together we may be part of the fullness of Christ's own suffering for us.

Roger Grainger
England

How Long Do We Have to Bring This Broken World to You, O God?

Lord God, we want to place ourselves in your hands *(pause)*;
We long to feel your embrace as you heal us and calm us.
We hear the world rage about us
And our hearts cry out in anguish –
How long do we have to bring this broken world to you, O
    God?
We can see no end to the wars, famines and disasters
And we share the pain of our neighbours, wherever they live.

Lord God, we want to place these neighbours in your hands;
Silently, we name them before you *(pause)*.
We ask that all those who suffer will feel embrace
As you heal them and calm them.

Lord God, sometimes all we can do is leave the situations in
  your hands.
Help us to know when that is what we must do;
Help us to leave our anxiety and impatience with you also.
Give us the faith and peace we need while waiting for our
  answers.

Lord God, there are other times when our prayers must result
  in action.
Help us to hear your prompting clearly
So we direct our energy in fruitful ways
And your love is lived out through our lives.

Lord God, as we pray for ourselves and our world,
We remember we all belong to you.
We are your creation and you love us,
You feel our hurt, you share our pain
And we know you can enfold us in your arms,
While you heal us and calm us.

So we place ourselves in your hands, O Lord.
Give us *your* eyes of faith –
Help us to see *your* way through the pain.
Give us *your* heart of compassion –
A heart that drives us to move and act in love.
Give us *your* welcoming hands –
May we embrace and heal like you.
Amen.

Ruth Sermon
England

The World Must Learn

Where were You, Lord,
The day they blew apart
My vision of world peace?

Where were You, then?

I can't believe
That the loving, all-powerful God
In whom I put my faith,
Couldn't step in,
Wasn't able to stop this horror,
Crush this evil.

I just can't credit
That You couldn't intervene, Lord.

So I ask myself, Why?
Why
Didn't You?
What has the world to learn from this . . ?

I look at the images of prayer,
See people on their knees,
Whole nations crying out to You
In a great cathartic, desperate wave of prayer,

And I have the audacity
To think
I know

The world must learn

Of Jesus.

Pat Marsh
England

The Real Enemy

My only shadow and misgiving is that I should be doing far
more than I am doing to leaven the country with the truth that
is so clear to me. I am convinced that the real enemy is enmity
against whomsoever it may be directed. Anger and enmity is
another form of fear and the most deadly corrosive of all joy
and peace.

George Maitland Lloyd-Davies (1880–1949)
Wales

Lord, Have Mercy

Lord,
We come to pray for peace.
But first we must face the truth about ourselves,
first we must acknowledge and confess our sins:
our incriminating complicity in conflict and violence;
our clever justifications of aggression and war;
our blithe indifference to the manufacture and sale of arms;
our cowardly laxity in calling government to account;
our perverse obsession with nationality and sovereignty;
our faithless concessions to the demands of realpolitik;
our convenient separation of politics and religion;
our ingenious evasions of the Sermon on the Mount;
our abysmal failure to put prayer into practice.
We are deeply ashamed of our actions and inactions;
they are undeniable and inexcusable.
So compromised are we, Lord,
so cynical about the world as it is,
so hopeless about the world that could be,
that we hardly dare to ask for your forgiveness.
But where else can we go?
Who else can we turn to?
Lord, have mercy.

Dig out the violence within us,
plant seeds of peace in our hearts,
and use us to 'spread the pollen of peace
throughout the land'.*
Amen.

Kim Fabricius
USA

Guide the Nations of the World

Almighty God our Heavenly Father, guide the nations of the world into the way of justice and truth, and establish among them that peace which is the fruit of righteousness, that they may become the kingdom of our Lord and Saviour Jesus Christ. Amen.

Edward Lambe Parsons (1868–1960)
USA

No Hate, No Bitterness, No Labels

A Hutu woman shades her eyes against the sun
as she looks to see if the children are coming back from school.
She returns to her never-ending task of washing
and then checks the cooking pot.
She has many children; three her own
And the other six, Tutsi orphans.
She lost her husband because he spoke for peace
and protected his Tutsi neighbours.
She gathered the orphans when the killing ceased
and now cares for them as for her own.
This is the hope for the future –
no hate, no bitterness, no labels;

---

* From the hymn 'O let us spread the pollen of peace' by Roger Courtney

217

simply living together as Rwandans,
each seeking the welfare of the other,
the past events, not forgotten but forgiven,
and a determination to live for peace.

John Johansen-Berg
England

Hatred Is Never Conquered by Hatred

Hatred is never conquered by hatred; hatred can only be conquered by non-hatred. Not to commit evil but to practise all good and to keep the heart pure. This is the teaching of the Buddha.

From the Dhammapada

I should dispel the misery of others,
Because it is suffering just like my own,
And I should benefit others,
Because they are living things, just like myself.

From the Shantideva

It Matters to This One

As I walked along the seashore
This young boy greeted me.
He was tossing stranded starfish
Back to the deep blue sea.
I said, 'Tell me why you bother,
Why you waste your time this way.
There's a million stranded starfish
Does it matter, anyway?'

And he said, 'It matters to this one.
It deserves a chance to grow.
It matters to this one.
I can't save them all I know.
But it matters to this one,
I'll return it to the sea.
It matters to this one,
And it matters to me.'

Author Unknown

Our World Needs You, Lord

Our world needs you, Lord. We are wounded and afraid. But you are our Father and we trust you. We trust you with our lives and the future of the world and we pray together that your will be done and that your love shall triumph over evil.

Give the leaders of the nations wisdom so that there may be justice and peace. Protect their hearts and minds so that they do not slip into errors of hatred and the cry for revenge. Lord, be merciful to your mistaken and misguided ones who perpetrate dreadful acts of war and terrorism. Help us to love our enemies and forgive those who hurt us. Protect the innocent and do not let more innocent lives be lost.

Work mightily, O Lord, to bring good out of evil. Use opportunities to bring change so that there will be justice and fairness in dealings with developing countries and a true regard for humankind. Lord, may your kingdom come!
In Jesus' name.
Amen.

Dorothy Stewart
England

Sharing Jesus

Every day the world is changing,
Science reaches into space,
From its studies it discovers
More about the human race,
Yet with all its power and wisdom
People still need love and faith.

Even though our skills develop
Children die because of hate,
Want and greed divide the nations,
Ignorance decides their fate.
Thousands yearn for food and water,
Fear destroys and strength dictates.

Yet we tell a different story,
Of a God who loves and heals,
Cares for all of his creation,
Shows in Jesus how he feels,
For we see his power and wisdom
In the risen Christ revealed.

Now today we are his story,
Through our lives his voice is heard,
Peace and hope and joy and loving
Are the message of his word
Spoken by his faithful people,
Sharing Jesus with the world.

Colin Ferguson
England

To Plan for the Future with Confidence

Let us pray that strength and courage abundant be given to
those who work for a world of reason and understanding; that
the good that lies in everyone's heart may day by day be

magnified; that we will come to see more clearly not that which divides us but that which unites us; that each hour may bring us closer to a final victory, not of nation over nation, but of humankind over its own errors and weaknesses; that the true spirit of humankind – its joy, its beauty, its hope – may live among us; that the blessings of peace may be ours – the peace to build and grow, to live in harmony and sympathy with others, to plan for the future with confidence.

Roger Grainger
England

Link Arms

Lord, help us to link arms with our brothers and sisters who are forgotten, wherever they may be, knowing that this is the task of the body of Christ. And in those we meet today, may we always be sensitive to those whom life seems to push down. May we remember to be with you in lifting them up – to let the 'nobodies' be 'somebodies'.
Amen.

Garth Hewitt
England

God Who Is Peace
A prayer of confession

God who is peace,
We stand by,
allowing our
governments
to proclaim war –
on terrorism,
on countries
whose leaders
we dislike,
on drugs,
on crime.

God who is peace,
we buy food
produced
by exploited labour,
goods crafted
by children,
financial products
profiting from
arms sales
and environmental
destruction.

God who is peace,
forgive us
for our silence
and complicity,
for our living as
part of an unjust system.
Help us
to forgive ourselves,
to know when
we have done
all we can,
and give us peace.

Clare McBeath
England

God Who Longs for Peace
A responsive intercession

God who longs for peace,
We live in a divided and broken world,
a world where people march not for peace
but to proclaim their sectarianism;
a world where people have lost faith in political protest
and resort to blowing up themselves and the neighbours they
   hate;

a world where soldiers are called peace-keepers
and bombs are dropped in the name of national and
  international security.

God who longs for peace
Give us the wisdom to see both sides of the story.

God who longs for justice,
We live in an unfair and unjust world,
a world where supermarkets get bigger and bigger
while local farmers grow poorer and poorer;
a world where the haves get richer and richer
and the have-nots have less and less;
a world where the centre of the industrial revolution
lies polluted and half derelict, yet still we do not learn.

God who longs for justice
Give us the courage to challenge our unjust systems.

God who longs for healing and wholeness,
We live in a world which is fragile and broken,
a world where species are dying and becoming extinct
while we continue to pollute and destroy their habitats;
a world where victims are forced to relive their terror
if they are ever to receive justice from our courts;
a world of vicious circles where the abused
all too easily become the abusers of themselves or others.

God who longs for healing and wholeness
Give us the love to persevere when all else fails.

In the name of the One who dares us to dream peace into
  being,
in the name of the One who shows us creative ways to
  challenge injustice,
and in the name of the One whose love embraces all.

Clare McBeath
England

Make Us a People of Peace

It's a world of confusion, Lord:
We are muddled in our thinking;
We are mixed in our emotions;
We are inconsistent in our actions.

It's a world of lies, Lord:
We deceive ourselves about our motives;
We mislead others with doublespeak and spin;
We exploit you as an agent of social control and suppression.

It's a world of greed, Lord:
We worship the idol of the market;
We hallow the false prophets of profit;
We reduce people to punters and nations to debt.

It's a world of vengeance, Lord:
We allow the wounds of history to fester;
We refuse the healing of memories;
We betray the living out of mistaken loyalty to the dead.

It's a world of violence, Lord:
We use the technology of terror to protect our interest;
We invest our children in the business of bloodshed;
We justify war as first strike, last resort, or final solution.

O Lord,
In this world of confusion, make us a people of clarity;
In this world of lies, make us a people of truth;
In this world of greed, make us a people of generosity;
In this world of vengeance, make us a people of mercy;
In this world of violence, make us a people of peace:
In the name of Christ
Amen.

Kim Fabricius
USA

Psalm for the Road

This is not a highway, Lord.
I had expected a road better used,
better paved, more signposts,
certainly companions on the way.
Did I make a mistake somewhere
and take a wrong turn-off?

This track grows steeper daily.
Yes, I admit it's very beautiful,
and the views keep getting better,
but it seems so far from the city.
I'm not sure where I'm going.
Can't you give me a sign?

What's that? Peace? Why, yes, Lord,
this road is full of peace. It hangs in the air,
it's everywhere. You mean that's it?
Peace is the sign I'm on the right road?

Well, thanks, Lord. That's good to know,
And shalom to you, too.

Joy Cowley
Aotearoa New Zealand

Listen

When the words that you've said,
the things that you've done,
have driven you far apart;
and the hurt
that you feel,
the anger so real,
is freezing your heart –
listen to him whose love alone can melt the ice;
listen to Jesus Christ, in whom all hatred dies.

Long ago, you've heard it said: don't kill anyone,
For God didn't make the world to be a killing place;
But if you nurse an angry heart, or put each other down,
I'm telling you, that's murder too – God's judgement you will
  face.

When the words that you've said . . .

If you want to be God's friend and have peace with him,
Remember that those who need forgiveness must forgive;
So let the Holy Spirit in, and break the barriers down –
Be reconciled and show the world the way God's children
  live!

When the words that you've said . . .

Jenny Dann
England

Balancing Act

Wherever nerves are strained to breaking point,
patience stretched and tempers frayed,
till triggers are pulled and bombs explode,
on both sides of battlefields,
    barricades,
    barriers
    and no-go areas;

May all people of faith and goodwill,
walk the tightrope that leads to peace
and keep their balance.

Wherever grudges are harboured,
grievances nursed or anger manipulated,
in the hearts and minds of the marginalized,
      oppressed,
      displaced or
      dispossessed;

May all people of faith and goodwill
make peaceful protests
and take positive action,
to swing the balance.

Whatever stumbling blocks,
       stone walls, vested interests,
       stubborn prejudice or vaulted pride
       stand in their way;

May all people of faith and goodwill
make new pathways
that lead to peace
and keep them clear.

Jean Mortimer
England

Prayer for Reconciliation

O Jesus, through your passion, teach us to forgive out of love,
    teach us to forget out of humility.
Help us to examine our hearts and see if there is any
    unforgiven hurt – or any unforgotten bitterness.
Allow the Holy Spirit to enter my spirit and remove all traces
    of anger.
Pour out your love, peace and joy
into our hearts in proportion to our emptying ourselves
of self-indulgence, vanity, anger and ambition.
Help us to willingly
shoulder the cross of Christ.
Amen.

Mother Teresa
India

The Path of Peace-making

Lord, I want to be a child of God. Show me the path of peace-making today. I bring my prejudices to you and ask that you will continue to convert me day by day and step by step on the way, so that I never build up walls of division but become one of those who show that in Christ these divisions are finished. Amen.

Garth Hewitt
England

Ten Measures of Beauty – Ten Measures of Sorrow

Ten measures of beauty God gave to the world
Nine to Jerusalem, one to the rest
Ten measures of sorrow God gave to the world
Nine to Jerusalem, one to the rest

So pray for the peace, pray for the peace
Pray for the peace of Jerusalem
Pray for the peace, pray for the peace
Pray for the peace of Jerusalem

You can greet your friends with the word 'Shalom'
Or you can greet then with 'Salaam'
But peace itself will never come
Till there's justice for everyone
And there can be no peace for the Jew
Till there's peace for the Palestinian too
And there can be no peace for the Jew
Till there's peace for the Palestinian too

So pray for the peace, pray for the peace
Pray for the peace of Jerusalem
Pray for the peace, pray for the peace
Pray for the peace of Jerusalem

May the justice of God fall down like fire
And bring a home for the Palestinian
May the mercy of God pour down like rain
And protect the Jewish people
And may the beautiful eyes of a holy God
Who weeps for all His children
Bring the healing hope for His wounded ones
For the Jew and the Palestinian

So pray for the peace, pray for the peace
Pray for the peace of Jerusalem
Pray for the peace, pray for the peace
Pray for the peace of Jerusalem

Ten measures of beauty God gave to the world
Nine to Jerusalem, one to the rest
Ten measures of sorrow God gave to the world
Nine to Jerusalem, one to the rest

So pray for the peace, pray for the peace
Pray for the peace of Jerusalem
Pray for the peace, pray for the peace
Pray for the peace of Jerusalem

Garth Hewitt
England

Prayer of Thanksgiving

For those who through the years have laboured for
    reconciliation,
for those who have put their lives at risk in the cause of peace,
for those who have ministered the gospel in all the churches,
for them all we give you thanks.
Their heroic courage and their persistent endeavour have
    filled us with new hope.

Source Unknown

Brighten Our Eyes with the Light of Peace

O Lord! Draw up the people from the abyss of the ocean of hatred and enmity and deliver them from this impenetrable darkness. Unite their hearts, and brighten their eyes with the light of peace and reconciliation. Deliver them from the depths of war and bloodshed and free them from the darkness of error. Remove the veil from their eyes and enlighten their hearts with the light of guidance. Treat them with Thy tender mercy and compassion and deal not with them according to Thy justice and wrath which cause the limbs of the mighty to quake.

Baha'i' Community of the United Kingdom

God of Compassion

God of Compassion,
You gave us hands to offer healing;
You gave us voices to proclaim your word;
You gave us feet to walk the way of salvation;
You gave us hearts to love without limits.
So in our living, speaking, action,
may we spread your peace;
not peace as the world gives it,
but the deep, lasting, inner peace
that comes from abiding in you.

John Johansen-Berg
England

Everyone Will Live in Peace

Call to Worship

Leader: In Jesus' day
war was always present.
Rome occupied the Promised Land.

Jewish kings were corrupt.
And religious leaders, pawns of the powerful,
cried 'Peace' where there was none.

All: **Today the military absorbs
a large portion of every nation's
budget.
Terrorism is a part of life;
'ethnic cleansing' a new phrase
in our daily speech.**

Leader: Yet God unfolds within us
a sacred vision of peace and integrity,
of people living in harmony
honouring the Sacred in us all.

All: **For the sake of God's peace in our day
and in answer to Christ's call
to love those whom we hate,
come, now, let us worship God!**

Call to Worship

Leader: Jesus came to bring Peace –

People on the sides: not Peace as an absence of war

People in the centre: but Peace as the coming of God's
dream.

Leader: We enter God's dream

People on the sides: when we listen and understand,

People in the centre: when we forgive and care.

231

Leader:	We enter God's dream
People on the sides:	when we remember those who die for Peace
People in the centre:	and those who work for Peace today.
Leader:	As we worship God,
All:	**let us commit ourselves to Jesus' Peace.** **May we bring His Peace to people everywhere.**
Leader:	Amen!

Betty Lynn Schwab
Canada

Peace-Making Is Risk-Taking

God of hope,
    what does it take to make me your peace-maker?
Does it take a greater understanding of international affairs
    than I have yet?
Does it take more time than I allow yet?
Does it take deeper confidence in my faith than I know yet?
Does it take a bigger circle of friends and allies than I meet
    yet?

Or are these simply reasons why I allow myself the luxury of
    patient inactivity?
Am I really waiting for a time that will never come when all
    my questions are answered and all my uncertainties are
    safely put away?

When you walked the dusty roads by Galilee,
   when you called and some came following,
      weren't the questions only just starting
         and the uncertainties only beginning to multiply?

Perhaps the heart of faith is risk.
Perhaps the essence of peace-making is risk-taking.
Perhaps I should stop my hesitating,
   and get stuck in!
Amen.

Neil Thorogood
England

Giving

If you can give
You can live,
And not count
Nor mount up
Another's debt –
You can forget
And let
Be . . .
For we
All must
Trust –
And to trust
Is to give . . .
And to give
Is to live.

Margot Arthurton
England

A Peace Prayer from 1946

Almighty and eternal God, who hast entrusted the minds of men with the science and skill which can greatly bless or wholly destroy: Grant them also a new stature of spirit to match thy trust; that they may use their many inventions to the glory and the benefit of mankind; through Jesus Christ our Lord. Amen.

Source Unknown

Repentant Combatant

My Lord and my Maker,
I have bruised and ruined my country,
Have mercy on me.
Pardon and forgive me, my people,
For the sake of real peace, forgive me
And accept me, brothers and sisters.

Sinneh B. Conteh
Sierra Leone

Evil Has No Axis

Evil has no axis
outside the human mind
inured to pain and suffering,
that's heartless, sick or blind.

Those we seek to label
are human, just like us.
We show our inhumanity
when language is unjust.

Christ is in our neighbour,
but hatred screens our sight
distorting who we ought to see;
compassion's put to flight.

God sow seeds of conscience,
then nurture what's been sown
within the soil of our remorse,
till love is fully grown.

Andrew Pratt
England

Draw Us into Forgiveness

Your love, Lord, is cross-shaped.
In a world of power politics, intrigue and military occupation
  you allowed yourself to be sucked down by the schemes of
    others.
You appeared so weak, so vulnerable, so forsaken.
It makes us wonder.

Your love turned things round the wrong way, creating
  astounding possibilities.
You saw that people and situations can be changed,
  not by force and fear,
    but by your willingness to give yourself completely,
      and by your invitation for us to do the same.

So you draw us into forgiveness,
  the forgiveness we can know and the forgiveness we can
    show.
Work within us and amongst us, Lord of the cross,
  that we may see your resurrection in our lives,
    our time
      and our world.
Amen.

Neil Thorogood
England

Let Hands Speak Out

Bolton Hospice opened in 1991 and, together with Anglican and Roman Catholic colleagues, I was appointed as the Free Church chaplain.

Twelve months later we held a first anniversary service of thanksgiving for the life and work of the hospice. A central focus in the worship was the moment when we remembered the lives of all those who had died during the year in the hospice.

> Having given thanks
> 'for their courage in the face of suffering,
> their spirit of hope and trust,
> the example of their faith,
> their quiet endurance,
> their laughter and their tears'

we lit candles and sang 'Kindle a flame to lighten the dark and chase all fear away'. Then we sang Fred Kaan's hymn 'Put peace into each other's hands', followed by sharing the peace with a handshake or a hug. It proved to be a most moving and significant moment for all of us, but especially for those who had been bereaved. So much so, that for the following year's anniversary service the unanimous agreement was that we must use the same hymn again. Its sensitive wording touched the need of the bereaved and of those involved in working with the terminally ill.

As each anniversary came round the hymn was used again and again. Some began referring to it as 'the hospice hymn'! But a number of us recognized that over the years an increasing number of Muslim and Hindu relatives attended the service. Bolton has an 8 per cent ethnic minority population. And to sing

> As at communion, shape your hands
> into a waiting cradle;

> the gift of Christ receive, revere;
> united round the table . . .'

clearly gave people of other faiths problems. Though held in a Christian church, and at other points having clear Christian elements, the service was not intentionally evangelistic and we thought we should try to remove such exclusive sounding words.

So I contacted Fred. 'Any chance you could compose a couple of new verses which might be more appropriate for an inclusive, multi-faith occasion, Fred?'

And of course he did! To those involved in hospice work Fred's alternative words are inspired and inspiring, a prayer of deep meaning.

> Give thanks for strong – yet tender – hands,
> held out in trust and blessing.
> Where words fall short, let hands speak out,
> The heights of love expressing.

And the fact that the last line of the second new verse spells Peace with a capital P –

> Put peace into each other's hands:
> the Peace that sought and found you

– still presents the challenge of interpretation to the heart and mind of the singer.

Jim Hollyman
England

Put Peace into Each Other's Hands

> Put peace into each other's hands
> and like a treasure hold it,
> protect it like a candle-flame,
> with tenderness enfold it.

Put peace into each other's hands
with loving expectation;
be gentle in your words and ways,
in touch with God's creation.

Put peace into each other's hands
like bread we break for sharing;
look people warmly in the eye:
our life is meant for caring.

Give thanks for strong – yet tender – hands,
held out in trust and blessing.
Where words fall short, let hands speak out,
the heights of love expressing.

Reach out in friendship, stay with faith
in touch with those around you.
Put peace into each other's hands:
the Peace that sought and found you.

*The last two verses of this hymn were written, and should be sung, as
alternatives, and not in addition to the two original closing verses –
which are printed below:*

As at communion, shape your hands
into a waiting cradle;
the gift of Christ receive, revere,
united round the table.

Put Christ into each other's hands,
he is love's deepest measure;
in love make peace, give peace a chance,
and share it like a treasure.

Tune: St Columba

Fred Kaan
England

World Wide Web

Our map-drawn world is a spinning blue-green ball
caught in a linear cage of grid references.

If a single line is broken
will the ball spin
out of control
into oblivion?

Or will lines
ruptured by violence
open the hole
which finally spills life
out from our planet
into mass destruction?

Lord, help us to remember our connectedness!

Marjorie Dobson
England

For Parents Under Pressure

God of Patience and Peace,
give us the strength and resilience
to be good parents
at trying moments,
in stressful circumstances
and on all our bad days.
When the baby wakes us
in the middle of the night
and we have to take turns
at walking the floor,

Keep us cheerful and calm.

When our children are out of bed
and up to mischief
hours in advance of our alarm,

**Help us not to sound off
too harshly or too soon.**

When they bicker before breakfast
or bounce into our bedroom
when we are still bleary-eyed,

**May we send them packing
without putting them down.**

When they pester us for sweets
at the supermarket checkout
and throw a tantrum when we say 'No',

**Keep us assertive
without losing our cool.**

When they assail us with unanswerable questions
at the end of a demanding day at work,

**May we ask for time to think
without pushing them away.**

When they argue about whose turn it is
to do the washing up,
or refuse to co-operate
in sharing household chores,

**Keep us friendly and fair
without giving up or giving in.**

When they sulk in a corner
or behind a slammed door,

May we know when to back off
to give them space and time
to come round without losing face.

When the pressure mounts,
our patience snaps
and we lash out
with hand or tongue,

Give us the humility
to admit our faults,
to them and to you,
to ask for forgiveness
and to carry on.

God of Patience and Peace,
give us the strength and resilience
to be caring and consistent parents,

That we and our children
may grow through your love.

(In a service where parents and children are worshipping together,
parents may be invited to say the responses printed in bold.)

Jean Mortimer
England

Give Them Your Strength

Lord Jesus, we are glad that you are here with us. Thank you
for our homes and our families, our friends and all the things in
our daily lives that make us happy. We want to pray for those
people who are not as fortunate as we are – families who mourn
the death of a loved one; people who are injured in wars or
terrorist attacks; people who are worrying about their friends,
brothers, sisters, parents as they face fear and uncertainty. Be

with them and give them your strength. Let them know your love surrounding them and holding them up. Help us to learn through all of this to trust you even more and to work for peace – in our homes, our churches, our country and throughout the world.

Dorothy Stewart
England

Christ-Selves

We pray, please let us be ourselves.
Break us from the patterns that conform,
Break us from the masks that keep us safe,
We pray, please let us be ourselves.

We pray, that we can be ourselves,
Beyond the chains of dutiful existence,
Beyond the boundary lines that others make,
We pray, that we can be ourselves.

Frances Ballantyne
England

Resilient and Resourceful

Families in remote, rural villages in south India are resilient and resourceful. Many of the children have polio or cerebral palsy.
The families, with the help of trained and skilled medical profession-als, often find their peace through the dedication of these people.

Virupakshi is nine years old. His left leg was paralysed at the age of three as a result of polio. He was luckier than many children in his area of south India because there was a local clinic where visiting staff could provide some help. There, his mother was taught basic physiotherapy exercises to release the contractures in his leg. Once this was done his family bought him a caliper made at the workshop associated with the clinic. This enabled him to walk independently.

Virupakshi's next problem was getting to school since the road from his house was very rocky. Undeterred, his mother got together with the local community to remove the rocks and make the road safe for her son.

Virupakshi has been able to study in the 6th standard. His ambition? To be a doctor.

Ruth Duncan
south India/England

A Positive Husband

This is a true story about a marginalized family with mental health problems in a south India village. The community lives in poverty. This is an example of practical peace-making for the family.

Ramalingappa is always smiling and optimistic. Thirty-eight years old, he is respected in his village, in Tumkur District, south-western Karnataka, and in the Public Works Department, where he monitors the progress of road construction.

He and his wife Mallakka, aged thirty, have three girls and a boy, aged from two to thirteen years. Their first male child died at the age of five months, due to severe fever and diarrhoea. Mallakka became very depressed which caused impaired mental health.The prescribed medication made her worse and caused incontinence. Chronic anaemia resulted in a loss of energy.

Ramalingappa became responsible for caring for the family, including cooking, whilst continuing with his full-time work. He became embarrassed at having to cope with a woman's work so he shut himself in the house to avoid criticism by the neighbours. Eventually he persuaded Mallakka to stop the medication. He encouraged her with an improved diet of fresh green vegetables and very tasty curries.

243

Non-vegetarian food was prepared to ensure that Mallakka had sufficient protein in her diet. Her health improved.

Eventually, Mallakka began to cook again and this made her feel good about herself. She gained in confidence and well-being. Ramalingappa used to tell her she was very healthy. He gained peace and encouragement from the fact that he was helping his wife.

Mallakka became pregnant and they had another daughter. Ramalingappa saw a great improvement in her health and he continued to encourage his wife as she took care of their daughter. The time came to give the child a naming ceremony. However, the stigma of mental illness meant that relations and neighbours would not visit the family. Ramalingappa spoke with his brother's family, explained the improved situation and invited them to attend the naming ceremony. His sister-in-law, who had not visited the village home whilst Mallakka was seriously ill, attended with other family members, which pleased everyone.

Ramalingappa and Mallakka have been supported by the Narendra Foundation, one of the local partners of BasicNeeds. Ramalingappa is well respected because of his experience and positive outlook. He is asked for advice by other carers who have family members suffering from mental illness.

When asked why he wants to help others, Ramalingappa replies, 'My wife is suffering from a mental health problem. Being a human being and because my wife has this problem, helping others is my life.'

Geoffrey Duncan
England/south India

Keeping Hope and Goodness Alive

Thank you, dear God,
    for women and men of all places and times who have
      refused to admit defeat.
When the power of evil has seemed unstoppable,

some have stood their ground and worked for justice, peace
and love.
When the currents of nationalism have run into dangerous
flood,
some have lived and worked against the flow by reaching
out in hope and trust to the other side.
When ideologies have delighted in branding some people as
scapegoats,
other people have lived out their costly opposition to such a
crime.
When war has come and passion has run high,
many have fought with breaking, wounded, hearts
and some have refused to fight in their struggle with the
enemy.
When a divided and broken world has seemed inevitable,
some have lived a challenging alternative.

Thank you, God of justice, peace and love,
for all these your servants.
Some of them we honour and remember.
Countless others have worked away unseen and unremarked.
But all, in their own way and with the opportunities open to
them,
have laboured to keep hope and goodness alive.
Thank you for them,
and for their living example.
Amen.

Neil Thorogood
England

A Peace Blessing

Living, Loving God, Creator of Humankind,
Bless each one of us as we go on our way,
individually or together,
with love and unity of purpose.

Loving Christ, Creator of Compassion,
Bless us as we strive to bring compassion
    into the search for global peace;
    bless us in our efforts to influence leaders
    and politicians.

Refreshing, Dancing Spirit, Creator of Vitality,
Bless and encourage us to engage in lively activity
    for peace and justice
    in global situations;
    to turn disappointments into challenges,
    to transform darkness into light,
    to root God-given,
    Christ-like ideals wherever we and other people walk.

Go in grace
with confidence
and know peace.
Amen.

Geoffrey Duncan
England

A Closing Blessing

May the God whose longing is for justice
and whose passion is for the freedom of all
strengthen us to work for all that makes for peace.

Jan Berry
England

Chapter Six

The Peace that Passes Understanding

God's Peace

We need to fill our hearts
With God
And with his love
If we would ever come
To live in peace.
We must forgive all wrongs
Although we find it hard
To see why evil tries
To crush our innocence.
We need to turn to God
Whose peace passes all
Our understanding.
It is too deep
And wide
And all encompassing
For our small minds
To understand.

Lesley K. Steel
Scotland

The Peace that You Alone Can Give

Risen Lord, in the peace that passes understanding, in the peace that you alone can give, I know your peace and I rejoice in your love. Grant that my peace shall not be the peace of idleness, of complacency, of possessiveness, but the peace of confidence that reaches out to all who seek.

Raymond Chapman
England

The Gift of Peace

Give peace to your sister
for this is a gift
to bring families together.
Give peace to your neighbour
for this is a gift
which brings unity in communities.
Give peace to your enemy
for this is a gift
which brings nations into agreement.
The gift of peace is precious
like oil poured out in abundance.
This peace is health and welfare for all.

John Johansen-Berg
England

You Are the Colours of the Rainbow
(The work of the redeemed)

You are the colours of the rainbow,
the thundering sighs of love,
the shaking of foundations,
the seething clouds above.

You are the people God has chosen,
from exile you are freed,
your common consecration
means liberty indeed.

You are the hope of every nation,
yours is to bring God's peace,
the reconciliation,
the prisoner's release.

Andrew Pratt
England

Shalom, Salaam

three letters: s l m
one word
the root of peace
for jewish, christian and muslim people

salaam, shalom
Holy purpose and gift
not only merely for jewish, christian or muslim people,
the Holy is not so narrow

we say peace, the word says more
the word paints Holy vision and decision
about where all the nurturing will lead

behind and beyond the word is Holy imagery
the word
   draws a completed building
   etches a debt repaid
   paints a promise kept
   it is a picture in movement
the destiny: encouragement, renewal, completeness,
     wholeness

shalom, salaam begins tomorrow, today
salaam, shalom speaks of tomorrow, today
shalom, salaam leads to tomorrow, today
salaam, shalom inspires tomorrow, today

this shalom, this salaam is Holy
the portrait of decision, design and destiny
with us, through us and for us, it is Holy action, too

John Ll. Humphreys
Scotland/Wales

251

Be My Guide and My Inspiration

Come, Holy Spirit of God, to be my guide and my inspiration.
Give me your peace, give me your empowering, so that the
promises made at my baptism may be fulfilled now and in all
my life to come.

Raymond Chapman
England

A Song of Peace

You are a song my soul waits to hear,
But you are far from me.
This wilderness is a dry wall
Which separates me from you.

You are a song my soul waits to sing.
My heartbeat will shape
The grammar of its words
With love's emendations.

You are a song my soul waits to chant.
It will sound over the night ocean;
Skirting shearwaters will add
Their gloss of love.

You are a song my soul waits to tell,
But enemies stir hope to silence,
Set you outside determined
Bounds of the daily.

You are a song my soul waits to pray.
Piercing language, it is a worship
Enfolding little meaning in greater,
Catching beauty in the energy of light.

You are a song my soul waits to feel.
Its shock sets my joy free for an
Urgency – an unimaginable simplicity:
Your coming in intimacy.

You are a song my soul waits to hear.
I empty space for the space of love;
Then I am known in the unknown
And loved by the God of deep peace.

Derek Webster
England

Enfolding

Enfolded in your love, O mother God,
may we be freed from fears
we dare not name or face;
may we release the tears
that we hold back
in case our hearts will drown in grief
for past or future sorrow,
and in your arms may we find peace
and strength to live each precious day;
there may be no tomorrow.
You made us to be loved and loving;
though it hurts when we reject your love,
you love us still.
Your arms outstretched ache to embrace
and hold us while you whisper:
All is well; fear not, all shall be well.
All we need do is take the gift
of love and grace you offer,
and lay our head upon your shoulder,
let go of all that frightens and confuses

and lose our fear and find deep peace
in your enfolding, loving God,
our Mother.

Helene McLeod
England

May the Breath of God Be in You
Kirisuto no heiwa ga

May the breath of God be in you,
May the fire of love we knew from the start
And the peace of the one who makes new
Bring you joy to the cockles of your heart.

Father Izumi Shiola (Japanese original)
English text by da Noust
Scotland

To Keep You from Harm

When enemies attack you,
when foes surround you,
when the rich exploit you,
when the powerful oppress you
may the peace of God,
the peace that passes understanding,
enfold you and keep you from harm.

John Johansen-Berg
England

For the Sake of Life

For the sake of life the face of truth will brighten.
For the sake of life the seeds of hope will root.
For the sake of life the way of peace will lighten
for those who dare to walk
– for the sake of life.

For the sake of life the fields are being seeded.
For the sake of life there's still growth in the earth.
For the sake of life we'll share with all that need it
the bread from common soil
– for the sake of life.

For the sake of life a righteous wrath needs power.
For the sake of life let streams of justice roll.
For the sake of life the springs of joy will mother
the newborn child of hope
– for the sake of life.

For the sake of life our God became an infant.
For the sake of life he lived and died for all.
For the sake of life the time of God is constant.
The kingdom is at hand
– for the sake of life.

Per Harling
Sweden

The Peace that Passes Understanding?

Surely not.
Or, at least,
Only temporarily beyond understanding,
Provisionally beyond understanding,
Not essentially or necessarily beyond understanding.
Surely the peace of God is, in principle, understandable.
Surely all we need is more facts about it,
Or the right words and concepts to describe it.
Surely it's only a matter of untangling confusions
And teasing out an explanation.
Surely all it takes is a better spiritual technique,
Or a more experienced counsellor, or a wiser guru.
Better yet, a mystical experience –
That would do the trick –

Then, surely, we'd understand the peace of God.
And when we die, when we are at peace with God,
Then, surely, we will understand the peace of God.
Well, won't we?
No, I misunderstand.
With the peace of God
It is not just that our understanding is limited,
It is that our understanding reaches its limits.
With the peace of God
We must finish with understanding altogether.
With the peace of God
Our understanding must be crucified.
With the peace of God
There is nothing to be understood.
The peace of God
Calls us not to thought or meditation,
But to gratitude and adoration –
And to practice.
We can understand what it means to say
That God's peace passes understanding,
But that does not mean that we can understand
The peace that passes understanding.
We cannot.
The peace of God cannot be understood,
It can only be prayed and performed.

Kim Fabricius
USA

The Peace Beyond Our Understanding

Let me clasp your hand and give you my peace
For your desires are deep and thin as mine.
These outstretched hands will waver and retreat
Behind the barriers of my fear. Winter
Grips the earth and chokes all warmth and friendship.

Mined the fields that fed where the children played
As the world works for the favoured few
Death is in the skull to poison the new.

Peace comes like a sword to slash contours
Around the centres of the weary brain;
To let the nerve ignite the heart. So raise
Your open hand to the peace beyond our
Understanding that feeds the human soul
And makes you feel again, gentle and whole.

Bob Commin
South Africa

Touches of God

Statue of Mary at Ely
golden-haired head bowed
arms high to celebrate
holy overshadowing,
holy abdomen.

Silver wire Jesus
dancing stigmata
in the side of my candle
blackened by a match,
weeping wax.

Finger-sized petals of clay
on a little pottery bowl
made by my son when he was ten,
the year he knew he was gay.

A trio of notes in *Spiegel im Spiegel*
reflected and re-reflected
in the mirror of a meditating violin.

Silence at the end of music
someone's breath
held still,

still

Geoffrey Herbert
England

Peace

The peace of the lark's flight be yours
The peace of the flowing water be yours
The peace of the forest's heart be yours
The feast of the sunset splendour be yours
The peace of the God of creation be yours
Now and always

John Johansen-Berg
England

Great Spirit of Creation

The God of all creation
embraces every cell.
The One who taught the stars to shine
feels for the dust as well.
A God of grass and sparrows,
of those abused or poor;
this God of humble majesty
attracts us to adore.

The Christ who came to show us
the way to love the light;
to show how God's amazing love
dares to embrace the night;

a friend who recreates us
and calls his friends to share
in making one the universe
by challenges of care.

Great Spirit of creation
exciting and alive,
enlarge our view of unity
so that the world may thrive.
One world, one reign, one people,
one universe at peace,
one justice and one righteousness
one joy that shall not cease.

David Fox
Wales

Remembering Zeist, Christmas 1944

However forgetful I may become as I grow older, I shall always remember that Christmas in Zeist fifty-nine years ago. Of course prior to the Lockerbie trial, few people would have heard of my home town, that quiet and genteel garden suburb with its rather splendid though unostentatious mid-eighteenth-century Moravian settlement. I lived there during my teens and when I was a theology student at nearby Utrecht University.

Recalling the feelings I had when German soldiers occupied Zeist and sang their triumphant martial songs in front of the town hall arouses even now an almost physical response in me; but life soon settled down to something 'bearably normal', except for the Jews of course . . .

My parents decided (after open and honest discussions with my younger brother and myself) to welcome into our terraced house a young Jewish lawyer, and managed to hide her without the Germans ever finding her. Later we also hid a political prisoner who had escaped from Belsen.

False walls and underground spaces

We built a false partition on the landing to create a safe and undetectable space for our hunted friends during house searches.

Later, when both my parents joined the resistance movement, we also dug out the area under the floorboards, between the foundations. It was there that we were able to store weapons and ammunition which were regularly air-dropped and which my mother – of all quiet, unobtrusive people! – then distributed to members of the resistance unit in our neighbourhood.

But then, in September 1944, came the battle of Arnhem and its failure. Any hopes of an early end to the war were dashed, and deep darkness began to cover the life of the most densely populated provinces of the Netherlands. It was the beginning of what came to be known as 'the hunger winter', when supplies dried up completely, virtually every shop closed down, public transport came to a halt, food coupons were worthless and life was reduced to what I can only describe as 'primitive'. Three of my grandparents were among the thousands who died of starvation.

My mother was the only one in our family who could safely go out into the surrounding farming country on her bike (*no* tyres!) to try and obtain food through barter – anything of even the remotest value was exchanged for food. Most farmers were sympathetic and helpful; but many of them were unforgivably mean, and intent on getting rich quick. On one occasion she was given one slice of bread in exchange for a silver brooch . . .

The 'darkest' Christmas dinner

The day was dark; electric power only came on for a couple of hours, arbitrarily. A few months earlier a faulty German missile had crashed and exploded not far from our home, sucking out all the front windows, which my father and I replaced with planks and plywood.

It was the darkest Christmas ever. All we had between us was one slice of bread, over which a strange 'battle' of generosity developed in which my parents wanted to give it to us boys, but we wanted mother and father to have it – they looked so alarmingly thin.

But then it occurred to us that you could break bread and share it round. It hardly came into the category of miracles! None of us was particularly religious or churchy, yet suddenly it became for each one of us a real Christmas, even though our physical hunger wasn't stilled.

I find it impossible to define or analyse that event now: between us we had almost nothing, yet, without wanting to sound pious or preachy, we had everything. We were as close to each other and as fundamentally aware of our shared humanness as we had ever been. Yes, we inevitably shed tears of deep emotion, but then we hugged each other as passionately as never before.

Peace on *earth*

Endless rows of theological books throughout the ages have tried to 'explain' the meaning of Christmas – I have lots of them on my shelves – but my gut feeling about the feast will always zero in on the miracle of women, men and children sharing who they are, and what they have, with each other with integrity and love.

That dark Christmas 'dinner' in Zeist, 1944, strangely became for me the origin of my personal commitment to peace and justice. *Not* pious peace but as the angels (whatever angels are) put it: peace *not* in heaven, but in the real world, *on earth*, the only earth we know!

Fred Kaan
The Netherlands/England

Sing the Song of Life

When the seed of hope is growing,
sing, sing the song of life.
When the Spirit wind is blowing,
sing, sing the song of life.
When the air and sea get clean,
when the drought of land turns green,
when the weak are loved and seen,
sing, sing the song of life.
When the word of truth is spoken,
sing, sing the song of life.
When the bread of life is broken,
sing, sing the song of life.
When the goodness is revealed,
when the covenant is sealed,
when the broken life is healed,
sing, sing the song of life.

When the light shines in the darkness,
sing, sing the song of life.
When the heart grows in the heartless,
sing, sing the song of life.
When I see the You in me,
when the 'I' becomes a 'we',
when creation is set free,
sing, sing the song of life.

When the hurting finds compassion,
sing, sing the song of life,
where the heart may make confession,
sing, sing the song of life.
When the lost is found and prized,
when our dreams are realized,
when God´s will is visualized,
sing, sing the song of life.

Into hate and into dying
sing, sing the song of life.
Into suffering and crying
sing, sing the song of life.
Into mistrust, doubt, despair
breathe God´s healing, love and care.
Grace is given grace to share,
sing, sing the song of life.

Per Harling
Sweden

Jewel of the Hebrides

Dancing waves of Tangasdale,
Sweeping winds o'er thrift and sand,
Nature's hand is all sublime
Where winter's chill or summer clime
Beckons the discerning traveller
To Scotland's Western Isles
At Barra – 'Jewel of the Hebrides' –
Reflections pink and purple hues
Of sunset skies
    framing bright shell-shredded beaches
    around sparkling crystal water
    of turquoise ocean deep

From causeway to ferry,
From Castlebay via Eriskay –
Outlined by surprise shafts of evening sunlight –
Head north to Uist, Benbecula, Harris
Or beyond to Taransay.
Enjoy the moors and downland,
Glowing primrose fields, cuckoos, gannets, sleepy seals –

All playing their part on this glorious planet,
   so relax,
    revive body, mind and spirit
    in these enchanting isles!

Wendy Whitehead
England

Dreamer at Prayer

God of creation, Designer supreme,
Our sensitive weaver of action or dream,
With praise we adore you; we feast on your gaze,
Endearing, unending, O radiance of days.
To God of the workplace, to God of all skills
We bring our thanksgiving, we offer our wills,
With you and your colleagues, let's work with our hands
To love and to cherish; to pray for all lands.

God of all union, all parties, all creeds,
Bring us to new life through being, not deeds;
In the name of the Godhead, the Spirit, the Son,
As God's healing leads us, may all become one.

God of the Cosmos, great God beyond time,
When limits beset us, or sorrow or crime,
Be close to support us; ordain us as thine,
Through grace and through wholeness may forgiving light
   shine.

God of the landscape, dear God of all life,
May you, our provider, forgive us for strife
For those who face drought and daily distress
Let your spirit guide us, the needy to bless.

God of the flatshare, the commune or home,
We pray for the rootless, wherever they roam;

Whatever their story, whatever our song,
Lord, bring us together – that all may belong.

God of all certainty, God of all trust,
Please take our confusions and turn them to dust;
Relieve us of stress – your hope to reveal
As seeds of renewal we discover will heal.

Source of humanity, help us to see
The vision of peace is ours to foresee;
Remake us and mould us – your dreams to review:
Let your vision guide us true faith to pursue.

Wendy Whitehead
England

Storms

My God
you are my rock, my bulwark and my strength;
when weariness and wine and worry
cause storms of accusation to break about my head
and the bitter stench of acrimony
fills the living room,
I think of you and I am calm
and comforted.
I cannot see the way ahead
but this I know, to this I cling,
however much the storm may rage,
and howling winds tear at the boat,
within is peace and calm and rest
and I can lay me down and sleep
and you will keep me safe.

Helene McLeod
England

Pursue Me

When I have thought on all of you
   my meagre soul can bear,
O God,
still turn my thoughts to you again;

pursue me,
   my relentless Lord,
to corners where I crouch and quake.

For your Name's sake.
Amen.

Art Addington
USA

God Is Our True Peace

So I saw that God is our true peace. He watches over us when we can find no rest and he works continually to bring us peace that shall never end.

And when, through the power of mercy and grace, we are made humble and gentle, we are wholly safe. Then suddenly the soul is at one with God, when it is truly at peace with itself, for no anger is found in him.

And so I saw that when we are full of peace and love, we find no striving in ourselves and are not hindered by the strife that is in us now. For that strife is the cause of our troubles and all our sorrow.

And our Lord takes our strivings and sends them up to heaven where they are made more sweet and deliberate than heart can think or tongue can tell.

And when we get there we shall find them waiting, all turned
into lovely and lasting glory.

So God is our sure rock and he shall be our whole joy, and make
us changeless as he is, when we reach heaven.

Julian of Norwich

Deep Peace

Deep peace, pure white of the moon to you.
Deep peace, pure green of the grass to you.
Deep peace, pure brown of the earth to you.
Deep peace, pure grey of the dew to you.
Deep peace, pure blue of the sky to you.
Deep peace of the running wave to you.
Deep peace of the flowing air to you.
Deep peace of the quiet earth to you.
Deep peace of the shining stars to you.
Deep peace of the Son of Peace to you.

Fiona Macleod (1855–1905)

Finally . . .

How can there be something deep called peace
in a stretched cosmos full of restless energy,
atoms colliding, light, heat, piercing
every part of God's holy dark

as stars in our time? Our world turns,
our moon tugs the sea's vest up and over
to slip back, modestly. Our children breathe:
'our hearts are restless till they rest in thee.'

Yet we yearn for something unimagined.
The pool that silences and quietly stills
an endless mirrored blue unbroken sky;
that moment before waking when we know

flesh is stopped and nothing will disturb
our contemplation of the dreamless nothing
that there is held perfected in God's arms.
We say, then, that the dead 'sleep in peace'.

These are analogies. Yet somehow we know
there is a peace that passes understanding,
so deep that matter longs at last to reach it:
elements work to a last iron heart in a dark

star. Solids condense from this earth's shadow
and become heaven. Angels are more real
than we could ever be and Christ's love
has texture and geometry. It endures.

It promises eternal rest deep in God's heart,
where we will be as God means us to be:
concrete, pure, refilled, remade, come home
to where the Spirit names creation done.

Anne Richards
England

Chapter Seven
The Prince of Peace

He Comes with Healing in His Wings

He comes to make an end of war;
He comes with justice for the poor –
Our Lord, our peace, our joy.
He paid the price to break the wall,
To end hostility and call
Us to a living hope.

He comes with leopard and with lamb
At peace with wolf and asp and ram –
Our Lord, our peace, our joy.
For the whole earth in him can know
The height and depth and in him grow
Into a living hope.

He comes with healing in his wings;
The leper with the dumb man sings –
Our Lord, our peace, our joy.
He comes to make all people free,
The broken whole, the blind to see
And grasp the living hope.

He comes to us as God on earth;
He comes to kindle love and mirth –
Our Lord, our peace, our joy.
In him all strife shall be contained,
All glory known, knowledge contained
In him, the living hope.

Tune: Cornwall

Adrienne Dones/Peter Birdsey
England

Messenger

Look out over fields and meadows;
watch the hills and far mountains;
wait patiently for the messenger.
When the day comes, how welcome
Is the messenger of peace,
the one who declares salvation.
The people will sing for joy
when God redeems them,
when he brings the blessing of peace.

John Johansen-Berg
England

Child of Peace

Child of Peace
   We give thanks for your birth;
   Shining with possibility
   A regeneration of hope.

Child of Peace
   We pray for your growth;
   In health and freedom
   With the love you deserve.

Child of Peace
   We yearn for your innocence;
   May we remember a time
   Before injustice was real.

Child of Peace
   We hope for your life;
   That it may be filled
   With all that you need.

Child of Peace
We ask for your blessing;
That we may become
Like the one who came for us.

Child of Peace,
We will work for your future;
That all may see
The holy child in you.

Louise Margaret Granahan
Canada

My Beloved: The Prince of Peace

Not from a solitude of prison or incapacity
But of high plains and wide skies,
My beloved comes to me.

Through a valley of unmown fields and cinnamon sun,
Where quails skirt their ways and white junipers grow,
My beloved walks with me.

Discarding a syntax of usage and convention,
In language bending beyond rulebound borders,
My beloved speaks to me.

An unquenchable music, housed in the motion of stillness,
Distils to this: *I keep you in the lock of love's arms,*
For you are mine.

Though you are where phantoms scourge and doubt gnaws,
Where death censors life and torments truth, look to me
And I will stand with you.

My enemies, deflecting love, decorating barbarism,
Voyeurs of suffering and intimacy,
Surround me.

But they see that we celebrate and dare not intervene.
A meal of new bread and good wine is laid. The
Beloved kisses and crowns my head – a

Space for love brings love. When knowing is breached
By eternity, when all days become one day, I shall find
The mystery of his uncalculating love.

Derek Webster
England

Immanuel

Immanuel, your name brings us peace,
Immanuel, your love brings us peace,
You came among your people,
   our sorrow you have known
Immanuel, God with us now.

Immanuel, your name gives us hope,
Immanuel, your love gives us hope,
You came among your people,
   our being you have known
Immanuel, God with us now.

Immanuel, your people long for light,
Immanuel, the Magi longed for light;
The glory seen in weakness –
Their baby on her breast;
Immanuel, God with us now.

da Noust
Scotland

Your Promise of Peace

Lord Jesus Christ, Prince of Peace, I claim your promise of peace that is not given as the world gives, the peace that passes all understanding. Come in the restless confusion of my days, come in the anxiety of my nights, come in the stillness of my prayers and let me rest in the assurance that all is well.

Raymond Chapman
England

Are You the One Who Is to Come?

Are you the one who is to come,
    or look we for another?
Will you arrive with doomsday drum,
    or peaceful like a brother?

Are you the Son who pardons sin,
    or look we for another?
Will you free us to breathe again,
    or with your judgement smother?

Are you the Christ to heal and bless,
    or look we for another?
Will you bring discord and distress,
    or comfort like a mother?

Are you the Lord whose love's free-range,
    or look we for another?
Will you embrace the odd and strange
    and altogether other?

You are the one, and now you're here,
    we look not for another;
Hail, Prince of Peace, who casts out fear,
    we greet you like a brother.

Tune: Dominus regit me

Kim Fabricius
USA

Jesus Lives!

Jesus lives, so peace is here.
Wars can cease and so can sorrow.
Violence is of yesterday.
Love can be the way tomorrow.
Peace with Jesus!

Jesus lives, so love is here,
free for all and always freeing
dying souls from death and sin,
freeing every living being.
Love of Jesus!

Jesus lives, so joy is here,
happiness beyond all reason,
pleasure making all things clear,
brightening each and every season.
Joy from Jesus!

Jesus lives, so God is here,
powerful love for ever for us,
all the help we ever need,
boundless theme of heaven's chorus –
God in Jesus!

Tune: St Albinus

David J. Harding
England

276

Prince of Peace
Thoughts on Leading Prayers for Peace

I labour for peace, but when I speak unto them thereof, they make then ready for battle. (Psalm 120:6)

O Prince of Peace,
week by week we meet to pray for peace –
peace in Northern Ireland,
peace in Africa,
peace in Jerusalem –
but week by week
war and hatred increase,
shoots of peace wither and die,
new conflicts erupt,
hope fails.

What is wrong with our prayers? we ask.
Aren't they heard?

Week by week we pray for the peace-makers
('Blessed are the peace-makers
they shall be called children of God')
but their efforts are outflanked by fear,
hatred, mistrust, the desire for revenge
among the peace-wreckers,
those who have given up hope,
who are driven to despair.

O Prince of Peace,
we believe our prayers *are* heard.
You have had patience with our human race for millennia,
are we to despair after only a decade or two?
Keep us faithful in our prayers.
Keep us nurturing the small seeds of peace (they are there).
Keep us praying for the peace-makers,
for the many who long for peace,

for the despairing who are tempted to become peace-wreckers.
Keep hope alive, keep us believing,
That at last your will may be done,
Your kingdom of peace come.

Louise Pirouet
England

Perfect Joy

The first divine greeting of 'Peace' was perfect joy. It was the word of salutation, the promise of the angels of the Nativity, the blessing to be given on entering a house, the word embedded in the name of Jerusalem. When Jesus uttered the word to his disciples on the evening of his Resurrection, the effect was more disturbing. This was not to be a return to the old ways, made sweeter now by the agony of loss that had been healed. Now they were still to follow, but in a different way. The broken fellowship was to begin again, with a Master known and loved but also glorified. He was giving them the great commission, the power and the duty to follow in weariness and persecution, suffering and death, to the final glory. The disciples, the learners, were to become apostles, those who were sent to proclaim the King. The night before he went to the cross he had warned them that his peace was not the kind of peace that the world knew. Now they began to understand that the peace of God was not in the outer world but in the soul. There was work to be done. The Easter message was to be proclaimed, then and for generations to come.

How often they must have remembered it, that promise of peace made on the eve of his Passion and the command not to be afraid. Years of trouble lay before them, though they did not yet know it. Years of wandering, privation, mocking, persecution and for some of them eventually a martyr's death. There were many times when their hearts were troubled and they were afraid, until they remembered again that their Lord was still with them. How often his servants in later years would remember the promise – missionaries far from home, striving against discouragement; weary workers for the faith in unresponsive slum dwellings; simple Christian people stressed and facing an unknown future. Peace was the message of the angels of the Nativity and in the world there was flight and massacre. Peace was the work of the Resurrection morning, to begin a new life and new responsibility. In the days of wars and rumours of wars there would be peace. A strengthening peace, an aggressive peace, breaking through resistance, demanding calm and assurance when the world had none to offer.

Raymond Chapman
England

Eucharist Preface for Advent
Based on a Church of Scotland prayer

Worship and praise belong to you, our Maker.
From start to end, you weave the web of life.
Dawn and the evening celebrate your glory
    until the day that sees an end to strife.
In Christ your Son are earth and heaven united,
seeking the promise of an age to be,
your new creation, all that we still long for,
    until the day when all the world shall be set free.

Taught by your Spirit, fashioned in your likeness,
we seek the city of your kingdom's peace
in light transformed, and earth restored to wholeness,
    and on that day, all want and war shall cease.
Daughters and sons of your redeeming purpose,
here we await the advent of your Son,
and sing your praise, with angels and archangels,
    today, as all creation's voices join in one.

(This may also be sung to the tune Londonderry Air)

Barbara Moss
England

Servant of the Lord

Holy God,
you have put your Spirit upon your Servant;
he will be gentle in his words and ways;
he will encourage those in despair;
he will lift up those who are crushed;
he will bring justice for the nations;
he will not rest until the whole world
finds peace that is your will.
Living God,
you have created heaven and earth;
you breathe life into your people.
May your servant
be a light to the nations,
bringing sight to the blind,
releasing the oppressed from prison
and bringing your shalom,
for the glory of your name.

John Johansen-Berg
England

Words of Peace

A man came down from Nazareth
With words of peace
Good news for the poor
With words of peace
Setting free the oppressed
With words of peace
A man came down from Nazareth
With words of peace

A man came down from Nazareth
With deeds of love
Hope for the humble
With deeds of love

280

Walking to a cross
With deeds of love
A man came down from Nazareth
With deeds of love

> *Deeds of love and words of peace*
> *Reaching out to the poor and the weak*
> *Bringing the hope of liberty*
> *Of starting afresh like a jubilee*
> *Of starting afresh like a jubilee*

Born down in Bethlehem
Angels sang of peace
Soon fled to Egypt
He was a refugee
Then headed up to Nazareth
Where his work would begin
Then down to Jerusalem
Where he died and rose again

Deeds of love . . .

Repeat verses 1 and 2

Garth Hewitt
England

Down Under Prayer for Peace

God of reassurance and peace:
I see the sun rising over the sea and setting over the alps
every day.
I see the barren branches bursting out in buds and then in
 blossoms,
every spring.
I see the *wai-ata,** the stream gently flowing,
always.

I know your keeping-coming love.
I know your never-ending love.
In the confidence of that love,
we can be accepting of one another,
we can open our arms;
we can be generous toward one another,
we can open our hearts.

Dwelling in that love,
we can have peace in our soul, home, workplace, city;
we can have peace in the world.

We can see in our neighbours the Prince of Peace.

* Wai-ata is the Maori word for a gently flowing stream

John Hunt
Aotearoa New Zealand

Bring Peace Among the People

When the song of the angels is stilled,
when the star in the sky is gone,
when the kings and princes are home,
when the shepherds are back with their flocks,
the work of Christmas begins:
    to find the lost
    to heal the broken
    to feed the hungry
    to release the prisoner
    to rebuild the nations
    to bring peace among the people
    to make music in the heart

Author Unknown
Australia

Broken Land

Let peace and love come down
Upon a broken land
Let peace and love and justice flow
And let's all take a stand.

The rising sun from heaven
Came down on unbelief
To lead us out of darkness
Into the way of peace.

   Let peace and love come down . . .

Upon a barren hillside
Peace flowed down like rain
Broken hearts were mended
Healing out of pain.

   Let peace and love come down . . .

He walked among the lonely
And the poorest of the poor
He gave His life to save us
He lives for evermore.

   Let peace and love come down . . .

Garth Hewitt
England

God of Grace, Listening, Loving God

God of grace, listening, loving God,
where there is any peace on earth –
peace among the nations
peace within communities
peace in our families
peace in our own hearts –
we know that you are its source,
that you are its wellspring: unfailing, steadfast.
For the peace we know,
fragile and flimsy and unfinished as it often is,
we give you thanks and praise.

You are the peace . . .
we are the negotiators of tenuous ceasefires.
You are the peace . . .
we sign pacts of non-aggression.
You are the peace . . .
we live in the nuclear stalemate
of mutual assured destruction.
You are the peace . . .
we settle for the absence of hostilities.

You are the harmony . . .
while we make do with silence.
You are the calm of concord . . .
when we are the treaty makers.
You are the tranquillity . . .
while we seem content with the absence of strife.

God of peace,
for the peace we hope for,
the peace that we yearn for, reach for, work for,
fragile, and flimsy, and unfinished,
as it often is,
we give you thanks and praise.

You are the peace, O God,
so take us in hand we pray,
and make of us –
each of us, and all of us –
the home where your peace may abide,
the channel where it may freely flow,
the seed bed for its planting and growth,
the womb for its gestation and birth,
the voice for its singing,
the hands for its nurturing, building, and sharing.

You are the peace, O God,
and for the peace that lives within us
who are made in your image,
fragile and flimsy and unfinished as we often are,
we give you thanks and praise.

In quietness now we come to you,
with our own prayers, seeking your peace for ourselves
and for those we love, and for the world . . .
(silent prayer)
In the name of the one we know as Prince of Peace
we pray, and now in the words he taught us,
we pray together:

Our Father . . .

*(The words 'You are the peace . . . we are . . .' are adapted from
a prayer by the Sufi mystic, Rumi.)*

Curtis Tufts
Canada

Atonement

Now is my soul troubled. (John 12:27)

The wounded men of every battle
and all the beggars and lepers of the earth
are festering and dying on my skin.
Every rape is a swordfish in my belly.
There are deserts and volcanoes in my lungs,
and millions of ripped and trapped animals
are howling in my guts.
Victims and torturers, be my wounds.
I want to be your blood brother with my body.
I want to shout Why? and hold you still,
and make a new kind of peace
at the eye of this chaos.
It will mean being racked beyond bearing,
until my bones crack apart
and all the hope and love bleed out of me.
Even then I shall not know that all is well.
We shall be on the dark edge.

Geoffrey Herbert
England

Peace

What is peace?
A word
A concept
A symbol
A dove?

What is peace
In the midst of strife
In the midst of war?
All kinds of war

Of guns and hate
Of division and scorn
Of lovelessness.

Peace comes
When we transform
Our words
Our concepts
Our symbols
Our doves
Into a life of peace
Lived in the Prince of Peace.

Claire Smith
Guyana

Keeping the Peace

*A meditation on the familiar phrase 'keeping the peace'. One way,
strangely, is to employ armed troops or wage war. Jesus, the Prince of
Peace, showed us another way both to keep an inner personal peace
and to contribute to the peace of nations. Prayer, obedience and
unconditional love of others create 'paths of peace'.*

Yesterday's paper had a photo,
of New Zealand troops, gas masks, guns,
boots and battledress.
A show of strength, going to keep the peace.
Bravo our troops.
Not all peace-keepers carry guns.
Ranks of these troops
occupy monastery churches.
Keeping faith, honouring tradition,
prayer is offered daily,
across the globe.

In church the troops are divided,
one side sings, the other responds.
At night, after the final prayer, all turn
to sing an ancient hymn to Mary.
As we waited for the opening chord,
I was reminded of troops,
well-disciplined, dedicated to their cause.
There are no medals or ribbons,
nor reports of bravery sent back.
Death is bloodless here.
But no less a death
that takes a lifetime.

Are territories lost or gained?
Is worldly power the goal?
Can they be dispatched to trouble spots?
Are there ceremonies held at dawn
to remember giving of life for peace?
We have little idea of this other war,
waged daily on our behalf.
The only weapon – obedience.
And the tactic simple enough.
'Thy reign of peace come,
here on earth, as it is in heaven.'
It is called keeping the peace.

God whose glory shone in the face of Christ,
grant us wisdom and courage
to keep our peace and the peace of others
without resorting to violence of any kind.
Amen.

Wendy Ward
Aotearoa New Zealand

Utter Vulnerability

When You
Were utterly vulnerable, Lord;
Arms outstretched
On that lonely cross,
Pain
Searing through
Your bloodstained form . . .

When at Your weakest
Then You were strongest;
Forgiveness
Intermingled with the blood,
Offering Your wounds
In sacrificial love
As You journeyed on
Towards the time
Of total surrender before the Father;
That point
At which the pain of letting go,
Completely letting go,
Became the redeeming moment
Of being free.

Utter vulnerability.

Total self-giving surrender.

Transforming us
To freely love.

Pat Marsh
England

A Prayer for Peace

All-loving God,
>> guard us from straying from your way,
>> keep us secure in your truth,
>> and give us grace
>> to accept life as only to be given.

We pray against all obstacles to peace,
>> recognized and unrecognized.

We pray for warmongers
>> that they may be prevented from provoking
>> military force or being provoked to destructive
>> and murderous actions.

We pray for diplomats and negotiators
>> that they shall not entertain war as an option
>> to cover their own failures.

We pray for political reporters and commentators
>> that they may insist on freedom to broadcast
>> all truth and themselves recognize and avoid
>> slick images of bias and vilification.

We pray for the unmasking of those forces
>> that seek local economic gain at the expense
>> of widespread insecurity.

Especially, Prince of Peace,
We pray for ordinary people
>> who pay the ultimate price of war
>> and so are deceived into taking war for
>>   granted,
>> to accepting propaganda at its face value
>> and tolerating the media's culture of privilege
>>   and violence.

God of Jesus,

>   commission your peoples
>   to help all to walk along the way of truth
>   that is none other than the only way of life.

This, by grace, we pray; and this, by grace, we will do

>   in the Spirit of Jesus who saw that God blesses
>   all who make peace.

Amen.

David J. Harding
England

Vision

God of time and eternity,
Fulfil your promise of peace.
May the people who walked in darkness
See a glorious light.
Having known sorrow in the past,
May they taste joy in coming days.
Send your Son, the Prince of Peace.
May he return to bring justice and peace
For all the nations of the world.

John Johansen-Berg
England

View Toward Westham House

Wonderful

>   the line of clouds

>   their tops

shining in the westward sun, they move
gustily eastward, in the eggshell blue
arena, just above the line
of the house-tops and the budding twigs of trees
not yet come into leaf.

Dun and dark, the apple-twigs make their own
chiaroscuro, their own jagged pattern,
this septuagesima, one
month from the shortest day,
and the sound of the wind is gusty
against the roofs and windows where I sit.

Counsellor

It uncovers the darkness, and the light
in ourselves.
It vouchsafes its vision to us, hands itself on.
It rises: it is about
to break forth into song.

Wonderful
          Counsellor

Disturbing the ether, it declares we are in the presence
of the **Mighty God.**
            Gusting upwards, it sings
of the **Everlasting Father**
            visible in the firmament
of the first and every creation.
            Growing calm again
it abates itself, remembering the manger,
            accords itself to the reign
of the **Prince of Peace,**
            Blue
sky: bright cloud, falling below the houses
as the sun falls.
            Twigs are still waving
from the original rushing of the wind:
the universe is spirit, is astir,
and in the calm, as in commotion, sings.

Brian Louis Pearce
England

All Hail

Hail is the Lord's
anointing, fit
for a Son. Cords
of hoar-grain hit

earth with globes of
tight-knit hoar-frost.
A kind of love
none else would boast,

proper to God
this Easter. Rain,
dry as a curd,
spares heads the pain

due to them. Sun
runs to dry them,
hail gone; yet none
who's known it come

drumming on him
can ever for-
get its Salem-
Salaam, Saviour.

A kind of rain-
bow rests, Son, on
hail, squall, and pain
of sin, now on.

Brian Louis Pearce
England

Go in Peace

Go in peace:
The Wisdom of the Wonderful Counsellor guide you,
The Strength of the Mighty God uphold you,
The Love of the Everlasting Father enfold you,
The Peace of the Prince of Peace be upon you.

And the blessing of God
Father, Son and Holy Spirit,
be upon you all this night and for evermore.

Armenian Orthodox Dismissal

A Blessing for Peace

May the Prince of Peace
enter today into our minds and souls

Helping us to transform conflict into peace
in our own small corner of the globe

May we never doubt
that good can triumph over evil
throughout the whole of creation.
Amen.

Heather Johnston
England

Index of Authors and Sources

Harris, Kelvin 124
Herbert, Geoffrey 60, 90, 105, 149,
    184, 257, 286
Herodotus 154
Hewitt, Garth 63, 99, 123, 151, 221,
    228, 280, 283
Hiscock, Alan 103
Hollyman, Jim 236
Hopkins, Gabrielle 55
Hulme, Julie M. 210
Humphreys, John Ll. 146, 251
Hunt, John 281

Jain Religion, The 10, 58
Jenkins, Jill 64, 160
Jewish Daily Prayer Book 21
Johansen-Berg, John 16, 20, 48, 51,
    53, 61f, 77, 83, 110, 127, 131, 200,
    204, 212f, 217, 230, 250, 254, 258,
    272, 280, 291
Johnston, Heather 5, 52, 294
Julian of Norwich 266

Kaan, Fred 237, 259
King, Martin Luther 17
Klimcke, Pamela 101, 185, 207, 210
Kooiman, Michael Jacob 71
Kownacki, Mary Lou 8

Lees, Janet 22, 123
Litherland, Alan 154
Lloyd-Davies, George Maitland
    216

Mackey, Elizabeth 114
MacLeod, Fiona 267
McBeath, Clare 5, 27, 93, 144, 221f
McLeod, Helene 54, 57, 143, 253,
    265
Marsh, Pat 134, 215, 289
Mortimer, Jean 65, 147, 226, 239
Moseray, Josephine 77

Moss, Barbara 40, 279
Muslim Faith, The 10

Okwaci, Rebecca Joshua 129
Orchard, Stephen 45, 107

Paget, Francis 19
Parsons, Edward Lambe 217
Paton, Alan 19
Pearce, Brian Louis 39, 40, 67f, 79,
    291, 293
Pencavel, Heather 98, 117, 160
Philpott, Val 83
Pirouet, Louise 277
Platten, Stephen 47, 90, 128
Pratt, Andrew 7, 14, 31, 53, 132,
    234, 250
Pym, Jim 17

Rayner, John D. 208
Reiss, Michael 104
Rhosier, Nia 198
Richards, Anne 190, 267

Sanderson, Lindsey 72
Schwab, Betty Lynn 230
Sermon, Ruth 58, 142, 213
Shantideva 218
Sheila, Mother, CAH 50
Shiola, Father Izumi 254
Smith, Claire 33, 56, 191, 286
Steel, Lesley K. 50, 249
Stewart, Dorothy 219, 241

Tagore, Rabindranath 200
Tapia, Elizabeth 77, 84, 205
Teresa of Avila 37
Teresa, Mother 23, 199, 227
Thorogood, Bernard 34, 38, 152,
    159, 167
Thorogood, Neil 37, 112, 156, 158,
    176, 195f, 208, 232, 235, 244

Index of Titles

Acknowledgements and Sources

Every effort has been made to trace copyright ownership but the publisher would be grateful to know of any omissions.

Chapter One: Visions of Peace

All Thoughts of Truth and Peace, Francis Paget, from *2000 Years of Prayer* © Michael Counsell, published by The Canterbury Press.

Alphabet for Peace: Wisdom Sayings, An © Derek Webster

Amazing God © Marjorie Dobson

Be Blissful and at Peace © The Jain Religion

Blessing, A © Bernard Thorogood

Break Your Sword, Mahatma Gandhi

Challenged to Reconcile © Clare McBeath

Choose a Life of Non-violence © Sister Mary Lou Kownacki OSB and Pax Christi, USA, www.paxchristiusa.org

Compline, translated in *The Prayer Book as proposed in 1928*

Daily Prayer for Peace, A, from the *Jewish Daily Prayer Book*

Faith in God, Mahatma Gandhi

Flowers in the Desert © John Johansen-Berg

For the Healing of the World © Per Harling

Franciscan Prayer for Peace, A, The Franciscan Tradition, source unknown

Fruits of Peace, The, Mother Teresa

God Help Us © Louise Margaret Granahan

God of All Creation © Per Harling

God of Love and Love Abundant © David J. Harding

Hands © Per Harling

Is This a Place Where Games Are Played?, Andrew Pratt © Stainer and Bell Ltd

Jubilate © David J. Harding

Life . . . Truth . . . Light Persist, Mahatma Gandhi (from *Mother Teresa's Prayer Book*, published by The Canterbury Press)

Lions and Cows © John Johansen-Berg

Live a Day at a Time © Christine and David J. Harding

Look Into a Person's Eyes, Source Unknown

Love, from the *Bhagavad Gita* © The Hindu Faith

Love and Peace, Source Unknown

Love to All, Source Unknown

May All Beings Be Happy © The Buddhist Faith

Moment of Peace, A © Heather Johnston

Peace: A Vision © Derek Webster

Peace Dream, A © Claire Smith

Peace in the World, Confucius

Peace Is . . . © Marjorie Dobson

Pray for Ourselves © Christian Aid

Propaganda, Martin Luther King

Sapling, The © Kathleen Davey

Thanks to God © Janet Lees

They Reply 'Peace' © The Muslim Faith

Three Steps of Grace, Source Unknown

To Be More Loving, Alan Paton from *Instrument of Thy Peace* (Fount Books, 2nd edition, 1983). Permission sought from Winston Press, the licensors, but address not traced and as found in *2000 Years of Prayer* © Michael Counsell, published by The Canterbury Press.

Universal Meditation, A © Jim Pym

Vision of God's Shalom, A © Clare McBeath

Visions of Peace © David Fox

We Have a Dream, Source Unknown, Copyright Control

Whatever Your Race, Your Colour or Creed, Andrew Pratt © Stainer and Bell Ltd

Work for the Peace of the City © David G. Cornick

You Can't Break My People's Spirit, Andrew Pratt © Stainer and Bell Ltd

Chapter Two: Circles of Protective Peace

All Will Be Well © W. L. Wallace

At the Ocean © Claire Smith

Benediction © Louise Margaret Granahan

Be Still © Lesley K. Steel

Circles © Kathleen Davey

Circle(s) of Peace © John Johansen-Berg

Come to Me © Martin Wallace

Cost of Peace, The © Stephen Platten

Cry for Peace, A – A Dalit Prayer © The Church of South India

Dealing with Differences © Jean Mortimer

Deep Peace, Traditional Celtic Blessing, Source Unknown

Dove, The © Bernard Thorogood

Earth Is Holy, The, Source Unknown

Evening Prayer for Peace, An © Heather Johnston

Focusing © Helene McLeod

Forgive Us, Lord © Stephen Orchard

God, When I Look into Your Eyes, Andrew Pratt © Stainer and Bell Ltd

Heavy-laden © Martin Wallace

I Am a Man of Peace, Mahatma Gandhi, Source Unknown

I Find Peace, Judy Gunthorpe © National Board of Catholic Women

It Had a Tune © Geoffrey Herbert

Jesus My Peace © The Revd Mother Sheila CAH

Larksong © Helene McLeod

Let Nothing Disturb You, St Teresa's Bookmark, translation © 1997 by Michael Counsell from *2000 Years of Prayer*, published by The Canterbury Press.

Lord Our God Will Be Our Guide, The © Jill Jenkins

Museum © Brian Louis Pearce

Olive, Acharavi © Brian Louis Pearce

Paraphrase of Christ's Prayer, A © W. L. Wallace

Peace Comes With Every . . . © David J. Harding

Chapter Three: Peace on Earth

Contemplation of a White Rose © Glenn Jetta Barclay

Convert Weapons into Goods © David J. Harding

Daisy Bud © Kathleen Davey

Envisioning Peace © Louise Margaret Granahan

Epitaph for Ground Zero, Anyhwere © Geoffrey Herbert

Finding Peace © Val Philpott

Flower of Peace © Elizabeth Tapia

Flowing Water © John Johansen-Berg

Gift, The © Zam Walker

Give Peace to Your People © John Johansen-Berg

God, Your Gift of Peace Is Precious © 1998 Carolyn Winfrey Gillette. Reproduced from *Gifts of Love* © 2000 Carolyn Winfrey Gillette. Used by permission of Geneva Press

Gospel of the Cross, The © Stephen Platten

Harmony © Elizabeth Mackey

House of Bread © Garth Hewitt from *A Candle of Hope*, Bible Reading Fellowship 1999

I Am Because We Are © Heather Pencavel

Inside Out © Margot Arthurton

Lord, Your Peace Disturbs Us © David J. Harding

Nature of Peace, The © Geoffrey Duncan

New Kind of War, A © Geoffrey Herbert

O God of Peace © Kim Fabricius

On the Road to Jericho © Joy Cowley

Pax © Brian Louis Pearce

Peace and Love, Josephine Moseray from *Friends Again* © 2001 Sierra Leone Council of Churches and © 2001 Churches Together in England

Peace Blessing, A © Geoffrey Duncan

Peace Finds Expression © John Johansen-Berg

Peace to the World © Elizabeth Tapia

Prayer for Life © Pamela Klimcke

Prayer for Peace, A © Derek Webster

Psalm, A: Unity © Derek Webster

Psalm of Peace, A © Elizabeth Tapia

Re-member the Future © David J. Harding

Remembrance Day © Kathleen Davey

Retaliate with Peace © David J. Harding

Return after Conflict, A © Derek Webster

Speak to My Silence, Judy Gunthorpe © National Board of Catholic Women

Swords into Ploughshares © Michael Reiss

This is a Day of Remembrance © Clare McBeath

Trees and Flowers and Mountain Springs © Per Harling

Voices for Peace © Basil Bridge

Weapons of War, Alan Hiscock © *Anglican Peacemaker*, October 2001

We Hope to God that Wars May Cease © David J. Harding

What Does It Take to Start a Fire? © Neil Thorogood

Where Homes Lie in Ruin © Janet Wootton

Chapter Four: Where There Is No Peace

African Child's Cry, The © The Gambia Unit of the World Federation of Methodist and Uniting Church Women

All-knowing God © Marjorie Dobson

Bless Those Who Mourn © Marjorie Dobson

Blood Brothers, Garth Hewitt © Chain of Love Music administered by Daybreak Music Ltd

Child of War © Margot Arthurton

Christ Among the Crucified © Anne Richards

Come Afresh on Your Holy Land © His Grace Bishop Riah Abu El-Assal

Coming of Peace, The © Philip Fryar

Dare I Pray? © John Ll. Humphreys

Destruction and Violence © David Fox

Do Not Say 'Peace' © John Johansen-Berg

Endings © Marjorie Dobson

Father, Forgive Them © Marjorie Dobson

Forgive Our Foolish Ways © Robert Anderson. Permission Sought

Goodness Is Stronger Than the Evil © Per Harling

He Is Dead . . . © Liz Davies

How Can I See a Single Face, Andrew Pratt © Stainer and Bell Ltd

Humanity . . . Inhumanity © Margot Arthurton

I Cannot Live As If Peace Is of No Importance © Geoffrey Duncan

I Can't . . . © David J. Harding

In Situations of Abuse © Zam Walker

In the Museum © Margot Arthurton

Jericho Road © Pamela Klimcke

Jesus in the Blackness © Ruth Sermon

Jesus, We Need to Talk © Neil Thorogood

Last Holiday Season, Anonymous

Longing for Silence © Martin Wallace

Lord, I am in Pain © Wendy White

Loss © Margot Arthurton

Messiah Journey © Geoffrey Herbert

Movements Against War © Alan Litherland

Naboth and the Unnamed Woman © Jean Mortimer

Neighbours © Geoffrey Herbert

New York 11/9/01 © Margot Arthurton

No Angel Song © Helene McLeod

Now Is the Time © Per Harling

O God, Our Words Cannot Express © 2002 by Carolyn Winfrey Gillette. All Rights Reserved

Only Way, The © Neil Thorogood

Peace Is Fragile © Stephen Platten

Peace – Like a Phoenix, Garth Hewitt © Chain of Love Music administered by Daybreak Music Ltd

Peace Prayer © Claire Smith

Playground Was a War Zone, The © Neil Thorogood

Prayers for a Hurting World © Clare McBeath

Chapter Five: Working for Peace

In Your Name © Pamela Klimcke

It Is Not Enough to Pray for Peace, Rabbi John D. Rayner © Union of Liberal and Progressive Synagogues 1995

It Matters to This One, Author Unknown

Keeping Hope and Goodness Alive © Neil Thorogood

Let Hands Speak Out © Jim Hollyman

Link Arms © Garth Hewitt from *Pilgrims and Peacemakers*, Bible Reading Fellowship (1995). Used with Permission

Listen © Jenny Dann

Lord, Have Mercy © Kim Fabricius

Lord of Life and Peace © Geoffrey Duncan

Lord Speak . . . © Geoffrey Duncan

Love Is the Only Way © David J. Harding

Make Us a People of Peace © Kim Fabricius

No Hate, No Bitterness, No Labels © John Johansen-Berg

One World © Marjorie Dobson

Our Broken and Divided World © Roger Grainger

Our World Needs You, Lord © Dorothy Stewart

Path of Peace-making, The © Garth Hewitt from *Pilgrims and Peacemakers*, Bible Reading Fellowship (1995). Used with Permission

Peace Blessing, A © Geoffrey Duncan

Peace-making Is Risk-taking © Neil Thorogood

Peace Prayer from 1946, A © Source Unknown

Positive Husband, A © Geoffrey Duncan

Prayer for Reconciliation © from *Mother Teresa's Prayer Book*, published by The Canterbury Press

Prayer of Thanksgiving © Source Unknown

Prayer of Rabindranath Tagore © from *Mother Teresa's Prayer Book*, published by The Canterbury Press

Prayer to Our Blessed Virgin © from *Mother Teresa's Prayer Book*, published by The Canterbury Press

Psalm for the Road © Joy Cowley

Put Peace into Each Other's Hands © Fred Kaan

Quilt of Peace © Elizabeth Tapia

Real Enemy, The © George Maitland Lloyd-Davies

Repentant Combatant, Sinneh B. Conteh, from *Friends Again* © 2001 Council of Churches in Sierra Leone, Freetown and © 2001 Churches Together in England

Resilient and Resourceful © Ruth Duncan

Responding to Our Neighbour's Need © John Johansen-Berg

Righteous Redeemer © John Johansen-Berg

Shalom for Your People © John Johansen-Berg

Sharing Jesus © Colin Ferguson

Someday . . . , President Dwight D. Eisenhower

Stand and Be Counted © Nia Rhosier

Stand Up for Truth and Justice © 2002 Inderjit Singh Bhogal

Ten Measures of Beauty – Ten Measures of Sorrow, Garth Hewitt © Chain of Love Music administered by Daybreak Music Ltd

Theft, President Dwight D. Eisenhower

Things that Make for Peace, The © Neil Thorogood

To Enter into Your Divinity, Mahatma Gandhi

Together in Peace © Pamela Klimcke

To Plan for the Future with Confidence © Roger Grainger

World Must Learn, The © Pat Marsh

World Wide Web © Marjorie Dobson

Chapter Six: The Peace that Passes Understanding

Be My Guide and My Inspiration © Raymond Chapman from *Following the Gospel Through the Year*, The Canterbury Press

Deep Peace © Fiona Macleod, from *Celtic Blessings*, compiled by Brendan O'Malley, published by The Canterbury Press

Dreamer at Prayer © Wendy Whitehead

Enfolding © Helene McLeod

Finally . . . © Anne Richards

For the Sake of Life © Per Harling

Gift of Peace, The © John Johansen-Berg

God Is Our True Peace, Julian of Norwich

God's Peace © Lesley K. Steel

Great Spirit of Creation © David Fox

Jewel of the Hebrides © Wendy Whitehead

May the Breath of God Be in You © Father Izumi Shiola. English text © da Noust

Peace © John Johansen-Berg

Peace Beyond Our Understanding, The © Bob Commin

Peace that Passes Understanding?, The © Kim Fabricius

Peace that You Alone Can Give, The © Raymond Chapman from *Following the Gospel Through the Year*, The Canterbury Press.

Pursue Me © Art Addington

Remembering Zeist, Christmas 1944 © Fred Kaan

Shalom, Salaam © John Ll. Humphreys

Sing the Song of Life © Per Harling

Song of Peace, A © Derek Webster

Storms © Helene McLeod

To Keep You from Harm © John Johansen-Berg

Touches of God © Geoffrey Herbert

You Are the Colours of the Rainbow, Andrew Pratt © Stainer and Bell Ltd

Chapter Seven: The Prince of Peace

All Hail © Brian Louis Pearce

Are You the One Who Is to Come? © Kim Fabricius

Atonement © Geoffrey Herbert

Blessing for Peace, A © Heather Johnston

Bring Peace Among the People © Author Unknown

Broken Land, Garth Hewitt © Chain of Love Music administered by Daybreak Music Ltd

Child of Peace © Louise Margaret Granahan

Down Under Prayer for Peace © John Hunt

318